GOOD
NEWS
OF
JESUS

L. William Countryman

GOOD
NEWS
of
JESUS

Reintroducing the Gospel

COWLEY PUBLICATIONS
Cambridge   ◆   Boston
Massachusetts

TRINITY PRESS INTERNATIONAL
Valley Forge, Pennsylvania

Published in the United States of America by Trinity Press International and
by Cowley Publications, a division of the Society of St. John the Evangelist.
No portion of this book may be reproduced, stored in or introduced into a re-
trieval system, or transmitted, in any form or by any means—including pho-
tocopying—without the prior written permission from the publishers, except
in the case of brief quotations embodied in critical articles and reviews.

International Standard Book Number
Trinity Press International: 1-56338-050-1
Cowley Publications: 1-56101-068-5

Library of Congress Cataloging-in-Publication Data

Countryman, Louis William, 1941 -
   Good news of Jesus : reintroducing the gospel / by L. William Countryman.
      p. cm.
   ISBN 1-56101-068-5 (Cowley)   ISBN 1-56338-050-1 (TPI)
   1. Jesus Christ— Person and offices. 2. Christian life— 1960 - 3. Theology,
Doctrinal— Popular works. I. Title.
BT202.C687 1993
   230— cd20   92-33566

This book is printed on recycled and acid-free paper and was produced in
the United States of America.

Third Printing

Trinity Press International
P.O. Box 851
Valley Forge, Pennsylvania 19482-0851

Cowley Publications
28 Temple Place
Boston, Massachusetts 02111

To the people of
Good Shepherd Church
Berkeley
whose encouragement and discernment
contributed much
to this work

Acknowledgments

My thanks to all who have contributed to the writing of this book, especially to:

the people of Good Shepherd Episcopal Church in Berkeley, to whom it is quite properly dedicated, since it arose and received its basic shaping in sermons and classes and conversation with them,

Judy Bare, Joe McInerney, Susan Loyal, Leslie Schlecht, Paul Colbert, OHC, Tom Schultz, OHC, and others who read an earlier attempt and helped with both encouragement and criticism,

members of the South Bay clergy colleague group with whom the book reached roughly its present shape and who were generous with their encouragement,

my colleagues on the faculty of The Church Divinity School of the Pacific, who care for both the academy and the church,

students in my course, Foundations of Christian Spirituality, in the spring of 1992, who read and offered advice on the first draft of the present version of the book,

Cynthia Shattuck, whose perceptive editing made material improvements, and Hal Rast, whose enthusiasm has been contagious.

The translations and paraphrases of New Testament texts in this work are my own, made from the Greek.

Table of Contents

A Reintroduction

At the heart of Christianity stands the figure of Jesus and the message he embodies. In the Greek language of the New Testament, this message was called *euangelion*. We traditionally translate that word as "gospel," but in modern English it would be more exact to translate it as "good news."

The book you have just opened is about this good news. It doesn't pretend to be a complete survey of the Christian religion. It only seeks to make what is at the heart of that religion available to us in a new way, in our own time.

I've called this book "a reintroduction." Most of its readers will probably already have some notion of what the Christian faith is all about. Many of those notions, I think, are quite wrong. I fear that the reader will bring to the reading of this book all kinds of assumptions that don't belong here, and I have tried to be explicit in rejecting some of these so that I can reintroduce something truer.

Christianity is about two thousand years old. In that time, it has developed many aspects that are related loosely, if at all, to the original message of good news. As long as these aspects of Christianity don't undermine or conceal the good news, there is no harm in that. In some cases, however, later developments have virtually negated the good news. In what follows, I have pointed out a number of places where I believe that common notions of Christianity conflict with the good news and must be abandoned.

Christian people continue to owe their primary allegiance to the Jesus who proclaimed the good news. Both within the church and outside it, people are now in a time of refocusing and rediscovery, a time in which they are asking what is really central to Christian faith. If we encounter conflicts between the good news and the traditions of the various Christian denominations, we must be prepared to choose the good news over everything else.

My book is one effort to express that good news in terms that can make sense today. There are undoubtedly other ways as well, and yet not everything that claims to be the good news of Christ actually is. You, the reader, must try to judge. Here are three tests to apply.

1. It must be related to the words and life of Jesus as we find them in the gospels.

2. It must be *news*, offering some element of surprise, some new way of looking at the world, even when you've already heard it a hundred times.

3. It must be *good* news, giving hope for the future, not merely creating new burdens and obligations.

These are alarmingly high standards to suggest to one's own readers. If I succeed in meeting them even to a degree, I shall be content.

Good News in Jesus

What God says to you in Jesus is this: You are for-given. Nothing more. Nothing less. This is the message Jesus spoke and lived.

But is it really good news? And for whom? And how does it compare with the messages you may have heard from churches in the past?

*T*here are other things God could conceivably have said to us. And, we may as well face it, most of us know forms of

Christianity that relay a message quite different from this one.

They say things like this:

"Good news! If you are very very good, God will love you."

Or,

"Good news! If you are very very sorry for not having been very very good, God will love you."

Or (most insidious of all),

"Good news! God loves you. Now get back in line before God's mind changes."

These messages may be good news for somebody. They may sound like good news for contented churchgoers—respectable, pious people who feel that they are already pretty much what God wants people to be. They may even sound like good news for people who feel they've been extremely wicked and now want to pay for their sins in full. But they're not good news for ordinary human beings—people who haven't been extravagantly wicked, but also know that they are far from perfect, at least by the standards of the respectable people of their world, and likely to stay that way.

Interestingly, Jesus preferred the company of just such ordinary human beings, people without the religious and social status that goes with a very pious and respectable life. He ate with "tax collectors and sinners"—not just once or twice, but repeatedly.

Presumably, they liked his company, too, since they seem to have invited him back.

It looks, then, as if the good news was originally good news for ordinary people, people who were not particularly pious nor particularly respectable. To them, God said in Jesus, "You are forgiven."

God might have said it more simply: "You are loved. I love you." This message is true, but it would have been ambiguous. It might have meant, "I love you because you're good." It might have meant, "I love the nice bits of you, but I really wish you'd clean up your act." It might have meant, "I still love you and would like to go on loving you, but I won't tolerate your behavior much longer."

Instead, God says something quite unambiguous: "You are forgiven." What this means is, "I love you anyway, no matter what. I love you not because you are particularly good nor because you are particularly repentant nor because I'm trying to bribe you or threaten you into changing. I love you because I love you."

As Paul put it, "While we were still weak,...Christ died for irreverent folk....God confirms his love for us, because while we were still sinners Christ died for us" (Romans 5:6,8). The point Paul is making (unlike some of his successors) is not that we are grotesquely sinful, but that God is astonishingly and unfailingly generous.

Jesus embodied God's good news not only in the words he said, but in the way he lived his life. He ate with ordinary, irreligious, "unworthy" people, and he included among his followers the kind of people a religious teacher wasn't supposed to associate with—such as women and tax collectors. He stood up for these "sinful" people against the religious authorities of the day, and finally, he even died to preserve the integrity of his good news. (I'll say more about Jesus' relation to the good news later, in the chapter called "Good News, God, and Jesus.")

Paul was saying that, in Jesus, we discover something fundamentally important about God: God's love takes us up precisely when we are least deserving of it, when we are least lovable. God expresses his love specifically for those who don't deserve it.

God's love can do more than this—and does. The good news is that it will never do less. When you are least lovable, God says, "I love you." When you are least worthy, God says, "You are forgiven." Take yourself down to your lowest, most unattractive, most undeserving state—and there is God's love for you, as alive as ever.

The author of 1 John put it this way: "This is what love consists of, not that we have loved God but that God loved us.." (1 John 4:10). It doesn't begin with us and what we deserve. It begins with God and what God freely gives.

Jesus told a story about this forgiveness, this love, this good news. (Luke 15:11-32). The story tells of a man with two sons. The younger, who would eventually inherit one-third of the estate, asked for his inheritance early, and the father gave it to him, leaving himself and the older son to live on the remainder. According to the expectations of Jesus' time and place, this younger son was supposed to use his share to set himself up in life, so that he would not be a drain on the family and might even be able to contribute to its wealth and prestige. Instead, he absconded with his inheritance to a distant place and spent it all on his own private pleasures—on high living and prostitutes. As a result, he became desperately poor and homeless.

The son decided to swallow his pride and go home and ask to be taken on as a hired hand—a poor existence compared to the way he'd been brought up, but better by far than what he was faced with now. He couldn't predict his father's response. But he had to try, anyway. So he prepared a repentant speech and set out on the long walk home.

As he got near the family home, his father caught sight of him and recognized him and ran out to meet him. He didn't wait at the house to receive his son with offended dignity; he didn't wait to hear the son admit how bad he had been; he didn't talk about making amends or doing penance. He did not even require a probationary period to test his son's sincerity. No. He just told the servants to prepare for a party, ran out the door, met his son coming along the road, seized him, embraced him, and welcomed him home.

That is what God proposes to do with you. You don't have to have been particularly bad. Perhaps you've even been a pretty good sort of person. But whatever you've been, this is how God proposes to love you—without the least regard for what you deserve.

2

Good News and You

What does this message of forgiveness say about you—or about any other human being? Do you have to be particularly good or reverent or devout or pious or respectable for God to love you so much?

No. God loves everybody, good and bad alike, with the same tremendous intensity. God forgives everybody equally as part of loving everybody equally. You don't have to be especially good to receive this gift, or even especially repentant.

Does this message mean, then, that you must be specially bad? If being the best person in the world is no help, should you think of yourself as particularly wicked?

No. You can't make God love you more that way, either. God isn't secretly hoping that everyone will turn out to be rotten so that God will have more to forgive. The point of the good news is not to tell us how bad human beings are.

Christians have sometimes turned the good news on its head in just this way. In order to magnify God's forgiveness, they stress the wickedness of humanity beyond all measure. They tell us that human beings never get anything right, that being human is equivalent to being always in the wrong, that everything human is fundamentally depraved. Of course, they don't seem to think *they* might be wrong or depraved when they say that.

Such claims are rather confusing and misleading. They don't seem to take account of all that we actually experience. Yes, human beings can be profoundly evil. We have seen plenty of human evil in the twentieth century, and it is usually committed in the name of high ideals such as nationhood or independence or religion or economic equality or the punishing of the wicked.

But at the same time we know that human beings can be astonishingly good: kind, responsible, loving, generous, even sacrificial. For all the killers let loose on our world in this century, there have also been the people who tried to shield the weak and risked their own lives to serve justice.

You don't need to be particularly bad any more than you need to be particularly good. God has no prior investment in either one. God simply loves human beings, whoever and whatever they are. You may be a rather good person—loving, responsible, generous, kind. Or you may be a person who has done much wrong to others and to yourself. Either way, God expresses love for you by forgiving you, by taking you at your worst, whatever that may be, and loving you anyway.

Does this good news mean that good and bad don't matter any more?

No. Anyone can see that they matter. Would you rather live among people who treat one another with respect and generosity or among people who only look out for themselves and care nothing for the people around them? Surely it is easier, richer, happier, and more blessed in every way to live in a society where people treat each other decently.

God's forgiveness doesn't take us out of this world and bring us into a new world without consequences. The forgiven are still living in the real world, the same world we have always lived in. Good and bad actions, love and hate, still matter very much—to you, to your life, and to the lives of those around you.

The good news only says that God's love for you doesn't depend on the quality of your actions. God has already loved and forgiven you at your worst. Much else depends on whether you act well or ill; but this one thing, God's love for you, does not.

And this is no small thing. It is not everything, but it's a very great gift. God's forgiving, never-failing love for you means that you have a place at which to begin in your life, a starting point that will always be there, no matter what you may have done to destroy or invalidate the other good things in your life, no matter what fears you have about your future behavior, about your ability to succeed, to be good and wise, to deserve well of yourself, your neighbors, and your God.

The good news is the beginning of something much bigger. It is the beginning of a new way of living in this world. In fact, it can be the foundation of living wisely and well.

But we shouldn't rush into that aspect of the matter. Christians are often in too great a hurry to get on to moral preachments. The clergy sometimes seem to think of themselves as morale officers, keeping us all on our toes, obedient to the local standards of respectable behavior, embarrassed about our shortcomings, shamefacedly cooperative with the lawful authorities, determined to do better in the future, and pumped up with the certainty that next time, with proper devotion to duty, we can win!

But this attitude forgets that *good news* is the central thing. We need to concentrate on the good news first and let it do whatever work on us God wants it to do.

Christians are repeatedly tempted to settle in with the culture of their day and place. They assume protective coloration. They agree to support the existing standards of respectability in return for a certain status and power in the community. They turn into guardians of the public mores, the very people who found Jesus so upsetting in the first place. From being the advocates of good news, Christians are always in danger of becoming the enemies and the suppressors of good news.

To escape from this danger, however, we have only to return to our sources, to the original message of love that brought us into being. Even when Christians forget, even when churches drop the good news for a second career in social control, the good news is still there: you are loved, good or bad, repentant or unrepentant, and you are forgiven all. Given time, this news will work surprising changes in your life.

The good news, moreover, is true whether you believe it or not. Too often, Christians have spoken as if God's love were available only to those who respond to it in the "right" way—by believing the doctrines of this creed or that confession, by following this or that rule of life (the more repressive the better), by having just the right kind of conversion experience, by being "born again," by belonging to the right denomination (taken by its members to be the only true church) or to some group of especially pious people, by reading the Bible in a certain way and drawing only the "right" conclusions from it.

Such teaching is a betrayal of the good news. Not because creeds or rules of life or conversions or theologies or pious associations are necessarily wrong. Some of them, in fact, may be admirable. They may help us think about what the good news really means for us. They may give us guidance in shaping lives that reflect the good news. They may open our eyes to new possibilities in our lives. They may support us on our human journey of growth and change. But God's love for us does not depend on our "getting it right."

"This is what love consists of, not that we have loved God, but that God loved us " (1 John 4:10). God's love is not conditional on anything. It is expressed in forgiveness. You can ignore or oppose God, if you really want to. It will probably do you no great good, but it won't deprive you of God's love, either. God's love has already taken any possible wrong or error or failure on your part into account. You are loved anyway. You have been all along. You will be all along.

It does make a difference, though, when you begin to suspect, however doubtingly and uncertainly, that this good news is true. It makes a difference not in God's love, but in your awareness of yourself and your world. The difference it makes takes the form of two gifts that we receive along with the good news and that grow along with our acceptance of it: a gift of honesty and a gift of authentic and appropriate self-love.

The gift of honesty. The good news says that God loves us no matter what—not because we have deserved that love by making ourselves pleasing to God, but just because God loves us. As we begin to believe that, we find ourselves free, for once in our lives, to see ourselves for exactly who and what we are. We don't need to be more beautiful, richer, stronger, wiser, more powerful, more in control, better, more perfect—not, at least, in God's eyes. None of those attainments will make God love you more. God cannot love you more. God has already given you all the love there is to give.

You can now risk taking a look at the you that God loves, at both your blemishes and your beauty. You can risk being *that* person, the one you actually are—not someone you once were before you first knew temptation, not someone you hope to become, with effort, in the future, not someone you've been pretending to be. You can be yourself in the here and now.

I don't mean that the present "you" is the last word on who you are. To be human means that we are always changing, growing, becoming something a bit new. There is nothing in the good news to suggest that you should stop still and become frozen in place. You are still in the process of being created, and you may legitimately hope for this process of creation to make some changes in your life.

But you don't have to run away from who you are now. You don't have to shun yourself or cut yourself off and try to turn into someone else. The future years of your life are not going to be an effort to escape and become someone completely different. You begin where you are by being who you are—a person loved and forgiven by God. You can now risk being honest with yourself because such honesty—even if painful and difficult—cannot do you any ultimate harm. God's love will still be there.

We are all afraid of honesty. We're afraid that we will find ourselves fundamentally and irredeemably unworthy and undeserving. When Jesus says, "You shall know the truth, and the truth will set you free" (John 8:32), we find that hard to believe. We work hard, instead, to avoid truth and hang onto our illusions about ourselves. But in the light of the good news, truth really does become liberating: knowing the truth about yourself means knowing the you that God loves. Even your worst qualities can no longer threaten to deprive you of that love.

What's more, knowing the truth isn't just about admitting our faults. Oddly enough, when we begin to be honest with ourselves, we may find that, in some ways, we think better of ourselves than we did. The veil that was supposed to hide our faults from us often winds up hiding our good points as well.

True honesty is never one-sided; it doesn't have a preference for the negative. But some of us have a false piety which tells us that, to be pleasing to God, we should think poorly of ourselves. We think we should concentrate exclusively on our faults, on our sins, on the moments when we have been less than perfect toward other people, on our failures. We confuse this kind of negative opinion with the Christian virtue of humility.

In reality, humility means nothing other than complete honesty about yourself. A genuinely humble person will be able to see both good and bad, both virtues and faults, both gifts and failings in herself. Since God loves you anyway, there is no virtue in making yourself out to be better than you are—and none in making yourself out to be worse.

Jesus, during his ministry, did rebuke some people for thinking too highly of themselves. Most often these people belonged to the existing religious or political elite. He gave the priests and scribes a very hard time because of their self-satisfaction and the hypocrisy by which they protected it. He would tell his followers, "Do what they say—but not what they do!" (Matthew 23:3). And he interfered with the normal functioning of their religion by healing people on the Sabbath and by disrupting the conduct of worship in the Temple.

If you are a religious authority of any sort, you may do well to reflect on whether you think too well of yourself. Jesus extended this kind of rebuke to the leading members of his own following as well, who were a new kind of developing religious elite! After Peter correctly identified Jesus for the first time as the Christ, he thought very well of himself, well enough to tell Jesus how he ought to handle his affairs. Jesus then turned on him and called him "Satan" (Mark 8:33). Even apostles have no guarantee of getting things right.

But with the less respectable, less "religious" folk, with diffident and marginalized people, with women, children, the sick—with people like these, Jesus took a different tack. He urged them to come forward. He treated them as having more importance than they probably ascribed to themselves. Mary of Bethany sat at his feet with the men, to learn what he had to teach. Her own sister was upset with her, but Jesus defended her choice (Luke 10:38-42). When Jesus' disciples tried to keep children away from him, he insisted on having the children brought to him and said to the disciples, "Be like this child. This is the only sort of person who belongs in God's kingdom" (Mark 10:13-16, paraphrased).

On one extraordinary occasion, Jesus was confronted by a pagan woman who wanted him to cast a demon out of her daughter. At first, he was unfriendly toward her and tried to get rid of her by insulting her; but she insisted on being taken seriously. Finally, she persuaded him. She won the argument, and Jesus admitted it. He let even his own self-assurance be rebuked! He told her, "For what you have said, go; the demon has left your daughter" (Mark 7:29).

Honesty does mean rebuking the proud. It also means new courage and confidence for the poor and diffident.

We may even find something still more extraordinary. The gift of honesty can not only show us a new picture of ourselves; it can actually show us a new and different picture of good and evil. In our normal human laziness, we think it's pretty easy to tell good from bad: what is respectable is "good" and what is not respectable is "bad." The gift of honesty will begin to make us wonder. It is possible to grind the faces of the poor and still be eminently respectable. Sometimes the respectable seem more interested in correcting the behavior of others than in becoming critical of their own.

Honesty makes us admit that what is loving is not always identical with what is respectable, and so it may make us rethink our ideas about good and bad. (I'll say more about standards of morality in the chapter "Good News About You and Your Neighbor.")

The gift of self-love. The gift of honesty means dropping pretenses—whether of your own goodness or of your own badness. You can begin to see yourself as you are. The good news says that, when you do that, you will find that one of the most important things about you is that you are loved. It is one of the most powerful things that can happen to any human being—maybe the most powerful.

Being loved changes us. Our lover gives us a certain dignity and beauty and importance that we didn't see in ourselves as isolated individuals, before discovering that we were loved. Our lover gives us a new grace, a new favor, a new value in our own eyes. To be loved and to love in return gives us new life, a new world to live in, even a kind of new self to live in that world.

It's sometimes fashionable in religious circles to say that the goal of religion is to get rid of the self. The good news, as I hear it, speaks quite differently. It says that the self—your concrete, distinct self—is God's beloved. Therefore, you have new reason to esteem and love yourself in a way that reflects God's love for you.

This will be a generous and inclusive kind of self-love. You won't focus only on what you consider your better points. Your self-love, like God's love for you, will embrace the whole person. You have reason now to treat yourself with loving-kindness.

The good news cannot possibly encourage abuse of body or soul or spirit. Later Christians have sometimes imported alien ideas of asceticism. Ascetics have practiced self-denial by refusing to honor the body's legitimate needs. There have been eras when no one who was not celibate, wasted from fasting, and filthy from refusing to bathe would have been thought holy. At times, ascetics have also isolated the soul from the beauty and affection and enjoyment that nourish it. They were so afraid that one might love something else instead of God that they nearly squelched the ability to love altogether and put in its place a hard and narrow kind of emotional life. Sometimes ascetics have even forbidden the human spirit to learn and think and exchange ideas and communicate with others, as if God does not want us human creatures to use the minds with which we are endowed or to know anything not previously approved by religious authorities.

Once we have heard the good news, we cannot accept this kind of attack on the self. We will learn, instead, how to honor the whole human being: body, soul, and spirit. There is not one pattern for everyone. What is too little food for one person is too much for another. What seems like normal exercise to one would be exhausting or harmful to another. One person's music is another's noise. One person's company is another's crowd. We are individually distinct, and we each have to find the right way to treat ourselves lovingly. That is what God, our Lover, wants for us.

When you know yourself as beloved, you will know yourself as capable of being a lover, too. By receiving love you learn how to be a giver of it. You are receiver of life—and giver. You are fashioned by the world around you—and, in your own way, you are its creator. As you shape your own life in the context of the world and in response to it, you are contributing a new shape to the world and enriching its life. On all sides, you are involved in a rich interchange of love, receiving and giving—an interchange that God has set in motion by first loving you.

The person you are now, the person you have been, the person you will yet be—*this* person God has chosen as beloved. As you begin to see yourself through your lover's eyes, you may come to love yourself differently. You may love yourself more honestly. You may love yourself better. You will not love yourself less.

Jesus told a scandalous story about a man who was employed to manage a great household (Luke 16:1-8). He was a careless manager and was dissipating his employer's wealth. At length, the rich man he served called the manager to account, ordered him to turn in his books, and dismissed him. At first the man who had been fired was terrified and full of despair, but then he became very attentive indeed to business. As he prepared to turn his records in, he called in first one of his master's debtors, then another. "How much do you owe?" he asked each of them. (A better manager would have known!) Then he would say, "Here, take the record and write in a fraction of that." Now they owed *him* something; and, by the rules of Jesus' day, they would have to return the favor when he was out of work.

At the end of the story Jesus tells us, "The employer praised the unjust manager because he had acted intelligently." Or perhaps it is Luke who is telling us that "the Lord [Jesus himself] praised the unjust manager because he had acted intelligently." We can translate the statement either way. The point, however, is the same. God loves you enough to be delighted when he sees you taking care of yourself— even if it should seem to be at God's own expense. God loves you too much to care exactly what you owe. God loves you with so much generosity and delight as to call on you to love yourself just as much.

Once the good news sinks in, you won't have to tell yourself lies about how lovable—or unlovable—you are. You can admit to both your virtues and your faults. The ultimate Lover has found you lovable, has forgiven whatever needs forgiving, and hopes to inspire in you the same gifts of love—a new affection and reverence and esteem for God's beloved, your own self.

3

Good News about You and God

T he good news points you toward a certain kind of relationship with God—perhaps not the sort of relationship you would have assumed or the sort you learned about
in church school. God has been variously portrayed as a patri-
arch whose main goal is to keep us in our place, a judge offended by our misdoings who is eager to punish us, a remote
power who deals with us capriciously, a maker of often irrelevant laws to test our obedience, and so forth.

The good news implies instead that God should be thought of as lover—as one who is deeply attached to you and wants to be with you, to make this love known to you, and to awaken an answering love. As John insists, "No one has ever seen God" (John 1:18), but this image of God as lover is the closest we will come. It is the image embodied in Jesus' life and teaching. As I've already said, God loves you no matter what. God does not stop loving you if you don't respond at once. Yet when a person does respond to God's love, it quickly changes the nature of their relationship. When two people become aware of the love each has for the other, then they know themselves as lovers and something new and powerful comes into being between them.

Paul describes this development as including three elements: faith, hope, and love (1 Corinthians 13). Once we have heard the good news and begun to respond, these three elements in the response shape our relationship with God.

Faith comes first. It is where the whole process begins. Faith means recognizing that the message of God's forgiving love is true. Our recognition may not be altogether confident; we may not be absolutely sure that the good news is true. We may only have a strong suspicion that it is so. Maybe only enough that we're willing to take a chance.

Faith, after all, is not knowledge. It is not certain, incontrovertible evidence, either. Faith says, "No one can be completely sure. But this is how I really think the world is put together. This is what I think lies at the bottom of it all. So I'm going to risk behaving on this basis."

Notice something I have *not* said about faith here. I've not said that it involves believing certain doctrines. It means believing the good news. That is all.

This is not to say that the classic doctrines of Christianity are irrelevant or useless or wrong. They are not any of those things. In fact, doctrines can be very helpful to us as we try to think through the implications of our faith. But faith doesn't mean believing in doctrines. You don't have more faith by believing more articles of the creed. The fact that you believe difficult or seemingly impossible things doesn't mean that your faith is strong; it may only mean that you're a credulous person. Faith, in its proper sense, means trusting yourself to the news of God's forgiving love—trusting yourself to it enough to risk the kind of honesty and honest self-love we've talked about above, trusting yourself to it enough to try living on the basis of it.

When you begin to say, "Oh! I think this may really be so after all. Unlikely as it seems, I suspect God really may love me in this way"—when you begin to say something like that, you are experiencing faith.

Faith, of course, doesn't make God love you. God doesn't love you *because* you now have faith. Faith simply recognizes that the love is there. Faith is like opening your hand when someone is offering you a valuable and desired gift. Faith is a kind of beginning.

God's forgiving love and your response of faith, taken together, make a *vocation*, a "calling." Your lover wants to be with you where you are; by faith, you assent to that. Together, you begin to discover a common history—a history that links you with God, an ongoing relationship, a partnership in love.

Vocation doesn't mean simply your work life or your religious life, although people often use the term in those ways. It doesn't mean just your choice of career. It doesn't mean dropping everything else to become a full-time "professional" church worker. It means learning to see and live your whole life as a partnership with God in love.

By faith, life becomes vocation, including those parts of it that are devoted to work, to play, to family, to friends, to religious ceremonies, to learning, to singing and dancing and sewing and creating art and building and making love and laughing and every other human activity. In all these things, your vocation is living out your love affair with God.

The life of faith isn't always solemn, inward, contemplative, or what we think of as "religious." God is not opposed to play. God has nothing against laughter. God is not disgusted by sex, having created it in the first place. A true lover wants to be with you as you are, wants to be involved in the life you actually lead—not just some formal corner of it, tidied up for honored guests but otherwise unused.

It is your *real* life that makes your vocation. Vocation is loving God and being loved by God in your *real* life.

Sometimes, that realization may make you uncomfortable. You may come to feel that there are things in your life that are incompatible with this partnership and you need to get rid of them. Or you may find that there are things you have been ignoring that you cannot ignore any more. Sometimes, you may begin to see that your partnership in love takes precedence over other concerns or goals you have.

But the solution is not to run away and invent a new life and vocation. Even if you decide to make changes, you can only begin from where you are. Your life will both change and remain the same. After all, you are unique. No one else can live exactly the life you have led and are leading. And you cannot lead anyone else's life. It is that very uniqueness that your Lover wants to share.

*F*aith gives rise to this partnership we call vocation. To sustain it, however, you need something more: *hope*. Hope is the expectation that God's love for you will continue.

This hope is not simple optimism—the expectation that things will go as we want them to. The example of Jesus reminds us that this isn't always the case. Jesus seems to have experienced a great intimacy with God. Yet, despite his prayer for deliverance, God allowed him to die on the cross and even to suffer a sense of abandonment. Only then did God reach down to him in death and raise him to new life (Mark 14:36; 15:34).

This is a very realistic story. It matches up with our experience of life. However strong our faith in God's love, we have to acknowledge that that love doesn't always work itself out, in our world, in simple or obvious or likeable ways. There are times when the going is easy and our lover is readily accessible to us. There are other times when everything is obscure and difficult, or painful and terrifying.

Hope doesn't deny this reality. Our hope is not that God will do for us whatever we wish, that our paths will always be smooth. Our hope is that God will always be our true lover. We hope that the story of our lives will be a story of growth in love—our love for God deepening along with our confidence in God's love for us, our partnership with God growing ever richer and more profound.

This won't always be easy. We rely on hope precisely because we don't yet find ourselves living the fulfillment we long for. We see our present lives as pieces of a larger picture, and we expect to find the complete fulfillment only in that larger picture.

At the same time, there are moments of fulfillment—partial, incomplete, temporary, but real—in the here and now. The good news is not just about "pie in the sky by-and-by." It is not an escapist tale about a future good that will make up for all our present misfortunes and sufferings. The good news is about God's enduring love for us, past, present, and future. Even if there are moments when, like Jesus on the cross, we feel abandoned, there are also moments when we sense God intimately present in our lives—moments that sustain and ground our hope.

Some of these moments may involve a quite direct experience of God's presence and love—what is sometimes called "mystical" experience. We are aware of God being with us in a quite substantial way, even though we may also be aware that the world is going on as usual all around us. Such moments of fulfillment are great gifts for those who receive them. That's exactly what they are—gifts. They are not necessary. They are not inevitable. They are not earned. They are gifts God gives to this person or that—perhaps seeing that they need them in a way that others don't. Or, as Paul says about all gifts, they may be given to one person only in order to be passed along to others (1 Corinthians 12).

Other gifts take the form of surprising reversals. We sometimes call them miracles, though that term might seem a bit overblown for most of them. We find that some of our plans are unexpectedly fostered, while others are stymied. We find that what we thought was an affliction in our lives turns out to have good consequences. We begin to understand our lives in new ways that make better sense of them. We find ourselves cooperating with circumstances of our lives that we previously thought we had to resist, or resisting those we once thought we had no choice but to consent to. We find openings into the future through a wall that had seemed completely blank.

Like mystical experiences, these too are gifts. They are in no way under our control. You cannot force God to give them to you by praying in a special way or fasting or doing the right set of devotions or believing "harder" or by making vows or by any other magical behavior, however popular you may find such efforts to be among Christians. Even if you could, you would be in danger of wrecking your love partnership with God. You would begin to see God no longer as your lover, but as your sugar daddy.

The signs of God's love, however, are already there in your life. If you look for them, you'll find them—probably extending back long before you knew to look for them. You will find them shaping your life, shaping your vocation, shaping you. And it is these signs, these gifts, these moments of fulfillment that ground our hope and keep us looking forward to its complete consummation in the age to come.

*F*aith and hope both find their meaning in *love*—now and always. As Paul pointed out, in the age to come there will be no further need for faith and hope. When we know God as well as God knows us, faith will be swallowed up in knowledge. And when our love affair with God is fully consummated, hope gives way to fulfillment. But the need for love and the enjoyment of love never cease (1 Corinthians 13:8-13).

The love we share with God here and now is the same love whose endless riches we look forward to in the age to come.

But what does it mean to love God? The phrase can evoke many different associations. For some, loving God means being in church on Sundays and holy days, saying their prayers, doing good to the needy. For others, it means remaining in a certain state of joy or even ecstasy. For some, it means abiding by the standards of respectability in their community. For others, it means studying the Bible or knowing theology. Any of these can, in fact, be vehicles of our love of God, but they are not the love itself.

(In fact, these things—especially the specifically religious observances—can turn into rivals of our love for God. They can become ends in themselves and cease to have any connection with the real God. More on this in the chapter "Good News and the Church.")

Love of God consists not in a certain set of feelings nor in a certain list of specifically religious behaviors nor in respectability or knowledge. This love consists, fundamentally, in sharing your life with God. You begin by recognizing how God has loved you, and you realize that that love, given by God, is the most fundamental thing you know about your own life. To see that and to begin living in light of it is what it means to love God.

Your own vocation—the unique shape that your partnership with God assumes—may take a conservative form or a radical one. You may be called to be a very pious person or a more secular one. You may be called to focus on prayer or on banking. Yours may be a vocation of power in this world or of apparent weakness. Any life shared with God is a life lived in love.

To love God, recognize that you are loved by God: loved when you wake and when you sleep, loved when you are at prayer and when you are occupied with work or play, loved in and with your loved ones and associates, loved when you live and when you die, loved when you do well and when you go wrong or fail.

Your whole life is potentially a partnership in love, a partnership in which God wants to share. To live in that awareness, even for brief and disconnected moments, is to love God in return.

Jesus told a story about a farmer (Mark 4:26-29). The man planted his fields and left them to time and the rains, while he went about his daily routine, day after day. The crop sprouted and grew on its own, shooting up, flowering, setting seed. Then the farmer started the harvest.

Living a life of faith, hope, and love is like that. We make our contribution to it, but the ultimate power is that of God, which gives the growth. This power works in and on us, not because we are doing anything great or wonderful or decisive—we are merely tending to our daily lives—but because it is the power of God's love. Yet we get to harvest the fruits.

4

Good News About You
and the World

One important thing about God's love is that it does not demand exclusive love from you in return. Oh, it does in one respect: God insists on being your only god, and we shall see why a little further on. But God doesn't ask to be your only beloved.

Quite the contrary, God asks you to love a great many other beings as well—in fact, the whole creation of which you are a part.

Early Christians knew that the good news of God's forgiving love wasn't altogether new, even in their day. It was implicit from the beginning, in the act of creation itself.

We certainly never did anything to deserve our own creation. That was an act of pure and free generosity. The God who gave us our first beginning in creation is the same God who has given us a new start through forgiveness. In both cases, God has acted from generosity, not from obligation.

In creating us and in forgiving us, God expresses love—and gives us a reason to love ourselves. We learn to esteem ourselves all the more highly by seeing ourselves through the eyes of our Maker and knowing that God has found us and the whole creation "very good" (Genesis 1:31).

As we come to value ourselves in this way, we cannot refuse to honor the rest of God's handiwork, too. As one could not love a painter and despise her most prized works, one cannot claim to love God and despise the world God has created.

John put it very emphatically in relation to the human creation: "If any one says, 'I love God,' and hates his brother or sister, he is a liar; for the person who does not love his brother or sister, whom he has seen, cannot love God, whom he has not seen" (1 John 4:20). What John says about the human creation applies equally to the creation as a whole.

*T*his means a number of important things for us—some that are related to the non-human creation and others that have to do with ourselves.

First, with regard to the non-human creation. Christians are sometimes accused of being indifferent to the earth, of despising everything they place "lower" than themselves on the scale of value, of justifying wanton waste of resources and pollution of the environment. In some respects, these charges are true, but by no means in every case. Certainly, they are not accurate as charges against the good news itself. But, in any case, they are particularly important issues for our own time.

Insofar as these charges are true, they mean that we have failed in our love of the Creator. No matter how much time we spend in prayer and contemplation, no matter how eagerly we look forward to the consummation of our love affair with God, if we leave behind us a creation that is sickened and dying because of our carelessness and greed, we are, at best, poor lovers.

The same generosity that created us created all the rest. The same satisfaction God found in creating us, God found in creating all the rest. We are one particular kind of created being among many.

According to the creation stories in Genesis, God gave humanity a position of preeminence, even of domination over the rest of the world. When Genesis was first written, that claim must have seemed a bit ambitious. There were still plenty of animals and other natural phenomena beyond the reach of humanity's power. Human beings felt they had all they could do just to keep the "natural" world from overwhelming them, from killing their domestic animals and reclaiming their fields and even their cities.

In our own time, however, we have begun to find how realistic Genesis is in this regard and how dangerous human beings truly are. Our power to dominate is real. But we must understand this power of domination as a gift of God's love. If it is a gift, we cannot use it to destroy other gifts, to tyrannize over the rest of God's beloved creation. That would be repaying love with hate, generosity with abuse.

Instead, we, the whole human race, have before us the task of learning how to exercise our power with care and responsibility as an expression of our partnership in love with the Maker. This will mean learning to respect the whole creation as coming from our Lover's hands, and it will also involve loving the creation for its own sake—its own wonder and fascination and beauty and complexity and even its terror and its lingering power to destroy us.

To love God's creation takes nothing away from our love of God. It even enhances it. God is not cheated of our love when we admire an orange, a pine tree, a panther, a dragonfly, a forest, a prairie, a waterfall, a shoreline. Even if we are not aware of it or deliberately intending it, the love we give the created world also returns to God.

God is rightly praised as Maker of all (Psalm 104). God is praised even as maker of those things that are alarming, dangerous, unfriendly to humanity—like Leviathan and Behemoth in the book of Job; for the whole creation contributes to God's glory and testifies to God's generosity and power (Job 40-41). When we love and reverence and praise the creation, we love and reverence and praise the Creator at the same time.

When we begin to understand the rest of the world as *creation*, as works of our Lover's hands, we shall also begin to have a new sense of who we are. We, too, are creatures—part of the whole creation, not standing over against it.

Some Christian teachers have encouraged us to understand ourselves in terms divorced from the rest of creation. They have spoken of humanity as being essentially spiritual. They have described us as spirits who happen to have bodies, or as victims of a civil war in which spirit and body struggle with each other for control.

The "lower" creation, by contrast, is seen as merely material. Rocks and plants and animals have no real relationship with the spiritual God, because only human beings can have that.

One result of such teaching was to reinforce the Christian tendency toward asceticism mentioned earlier. The idea of human beings as essentially "spiritual" encouraged Christians to see their own bodies as enemies or, at best, as tools of the spirit.

It is vital for us to reject such thinking—vital because it keeps us from hearing and receiving and rejoicing in the good news. God loves us here and now, as we are, no matter what—body, soul, and spirit together.

To be spiritual is not enough for human beings. It's not enough to *make* us human beings. Human beings are a wonderful, alarming, complex, confusing mixture of body, soul, and spirit.

This does not make us altogether different from the rest of the creatures. We are matter, as they are matter. Many of them have life and its accompanying drives, just as we do.

Some of them even reason, to some extent, as we do. We are parts of the same whole.

We won't be able to love ourselves without loving the world around us. We won't be able to love the world around us without loving ourselves.

We must particularly learn to love those aspects of ourselves that we have sometimes dismissed as too close to the "lower" orders of creation—above all our bodily selves, including our sexual selves.

Even when Christians have not judged the body as evil, they have tended to see it as no more than an instrument of the human spirit. If the God who loves us is really the same as the Creator, then we should learn how to take our bodies seriously, how to accept them as full partners in our humanity, not merely as servants of the spirit or as miscreants to be punished. The body makes us aware of our finitude and is sometimes a source of pain. It also makes us aware of the world around us and can be a source of delight.

Nowhere is the body more problematic for the Christian tradition than in the greatest of its delights—sex. Despite the testimony of Genesis that God created sex, we have often been suspicious of it. Some have argued—correctly, I think— that this suspicion has helped justify the subordination of women and of non-white peoples, whom the church fathers regarded as more fleshly, more material, less rational, and more sexual than themselves. Very likely, it is also a principal reason for the antagonism many people feel toward homo-

sexual persons, because they remind us that all human beings are sexual.

Some Christians have rejected sex absolutely, while many
more have defined sexual activity as a mark of religiously inferior people. Even those Christians who have accepted sexuality as, in some sense, a divine gift usually hedge it about
with as many prohibitions as possible. One has the clear im-
pression that, for them, it is basically a bad thing that can be
tolerated only within certain narrowly defined limits. To treat
sex in this way is to reject a distinct and important sign of
God's graciousness toward us.

I don't wish to suggest that the body and sexuality are always good. They are part of being human, like every other
aspect of our lives. We can do good or harm with them. Sexual acts, like all human acts, are subject to the criterion of
love that I'll discuss further on.

I do mean to say that we need to understand ourselves as
an integral part of the creation. We are not lost spirits from
some "better," "purer" realm, accidentally caught in the mire
of this fleshly, material world. We are living in precisely the
world where we belong, the world we were created to live
in. And God loves us as God made us—creatures of body and
soul as much as spirit.

We cannot love our Maker and be, at the same time, fundamentally in revolt against the way we are made. Such a revolt implies that we do not, in fact, trust God's love, that we
have not believed the good news, that we have no hope of
present or future fulfillment—that we have no partnership
with God, after all.

*J*esus told a story about a shepherd who had one hundred sheep (Luke 15:1-7). One of them got lost, and the shepherd—in what sounds like a foolhardy move—left the other ninety-nine exposed and defenseless on the hills while he went off looking for the one that had gotten lost. When he found it, he was more excited about that one than about the ninety-nine others.

God doesn't care about status. God doesn't see the world in terms of "higher" and "lower" creatures. God doesn't see human beings in terms of "higher" and "lower" natures. Or, if God does, it is the "lower" that God cares the more for. The good, sensible, obedient ninety-nine sheep are less important to God than the weak, silly, straying *one*.

*T*he time has come for those who hear the good news to reconceive both ourselves and the rest of creation. We are all elements in God's marvelous handiwork: the whole, complex human being and every other creature as well.

The future must have room for all of us, insofar as that lies within human power. We can contribute to that by revising our perception of humanity to include fully all those people and all those aspects of ourselves we have ignored or slighted in the past. We can do our part by revising our perception of ourselves to emphasize that we are one with the whole creation. We can contribute by revising our perception of the rest of the creation to emphasize our common kinship.

Loving God is not an exclusive act. It also calls you to love what God loves: your whole self, body, soul, and spirit, and the world around you in its full and grand diversity.

5

Good News About You and Your Neighbor

The good news you've heard about God's love for you is not for you alone. God has extended the same guarantee of love to every other human being in exactly the same terms—to the person you love best, the person you dislike most, the person closest to you and the person most remote, the person who deserves such love more than you do and the person who deserves it less.

To make the same point a little differently: every other human being is in the same position before God as you are. This has a great deal to say about how we regard one another and how we are to treat one another.

Jesus set up two fundamental principles of human behavior that follow from the good news. He found them in the scriptures of Israel, but he elevated them to a new prominence as the foundation of all human behavior.

The first of these principles is: Love God with your whole self (Matthew 22:37, quoting Deuteronomy 6:5). We've already talked a little about what it means to love God. Once we've heard the good news, it makes sense to say, "Love God with your whole self." It means recognizing that everything you are is founded ultimately on God's love and God's gifts.

This commandment doesn't mean loving God to the exclusion of everything or everyone else. People sometimes read this as a very "religious" commandment, directing us to abandon the world and think of nothing but God or do nothing but pray. But God doesn't ask that of us. In fact, Jesus' second commandment, which he drew out of another book in the scriptures of Israel and connected with the first, specifically commands us to love some persons other than God.

This second great principle is: Love your neighbor and yourself equally (Matthew 22:39, quoting Leviticus 19:18). Nothing in the scriptures of Israel connects these two commandments with each other. According to most of the gospel accounts, it was Jesus himself who linked them and made them authoritative for his followers.

The way the second principle is actually phrased in Scripture is a bit different from the way I've introduced it. It runs:

"Love your neighbor *as* yourself." This means, as I put it above, "Love your neighbor and yourself equally." Despite the plain meaning of the words, however, there is a long Christian tradition of misinterpreting them and turning them into something quite different. For many of us, they seem to mean, "Love your neighbor *instead* of yourself."

This is not just a distorted reading of the text, but a harmful one. Harmful for two reasons: first, it denies the good news itself by suggesting that your neighbor is more important than you are in God's eyes; second, it undercuts authentic love of neighbor by setting aside the standard Jesus set up for it. I'll say a little more about each of these points.

First, as I've already shown, one great thing the good news does for us is to tell us that we are loved no matter what. It shows us ourselves through our lover's eyes. Even if we couldn't see ourselves as lovable before, we must do so now. We cannot help it. To say that you should not love yourself is to make the good news false, to imply that God's love for us is a fake, that God was only claiming to love us in order to get us to do something God wanted us to do.

God's love for us really does call us into a new love for ourselves—not on the basis of our being deserving or right or perfect or better than others, but on the basis of our being loved by a great and worthy lover.

Second, it is impossible for you to love your neighbor instead of yourself anyway. The idea has a certain appeal to it; it sounds terribly idealistic and devout and heroic and self-sacrificial. But it is a mirage, a false ideal, even—improbable though it must seem—a self-centered kind of piety.

43

The notion of loving your neighbor instead of yourself is a mirage because it cannot really work. People who do not love themselves with honesty and integrity cannot love anybody else either. We notice that false self-love—arrogance and selfishness and egotism—gets in the way of loving others, and we suppose that all self-love does so. But this isn't true. What gets in the way of loving others is not self-love, but the lies we've based it on.

If you love yourself because you tell yourself that you are good and beautiful and wise and talented and therefore deserving of love, you will dismiss anyone you think is less deserving and feel embarrassed and resentful in the presence of anyone you think of as more deserving. Either way, you are competing with the people around you, not loving them. With a true, honest, authentic self-love, however, a love based not on your own deserts, but on the fact that you are loved, you can risk loving others, for you will see them as lovable in the same way that you are.

The notion of loving your neighbor instead of yourself is also a false ideal, a self-defeating goal. Love makes love. Being loved is what makes us able to love. And it makes us able to love first by enabling us to love ourselves without lies, without fancy window-dressing, and without having to think ill of someone else in the process. When the neighbor is no longer our rival, we can love the neighbor, too.

Unless we love ourselves, we will find we have no love to give our neighbor either. Instead, we'll try to pass other things off as love—ugly things, things like manipulation, guilt, repression, arbitrary restriction, disenfranchisement. Is there anyone who has not at some time suffered some such cruelty in the name of love? Sometimes the workers of such cruelty use the word "love" with complete and open cynicism; often, they don't know the difference, having "loved" themselves as badly as they "loved" you.

What's more, the notion of loving your neighbor instead of yourself, however unselfish it may sound, usually turns out to be a self-centered, self-regarding kind of piety. It is one more way to try to earn God's love. You propose to be so good, so bountiful, so generous that you will accept nothing for yourself, that you will live only in order to give love away to others. Does it sound noble? No. It sounds inhuman. Only God is rich enough to live that way, and yet even God doesn't refuse to be loved. No human being is as rich as God. If you do not allow your stores to be replenished, you will soon have nothing to give.

Try as hard as you wish, you cannot love another *instead* of yourself. You cannot love another *better* than you love yourself. The highest legitimately human goal is to love your neighbor *as* yourself. Then, as you learn to love yourself well, you can love your neighbor well, too. By "well," I mean honestly and generously, without lies or pretense, without false humility or affectation or sentimentality, without pomposity or arrogance.

To love well means to love people as they are, without illusions. We all have our good features and our bad. We all have growing and learning that we could do. But we have to do them ourselves—with the help of others but without putting others in charge of what is our own responsibility. To love means leaving people free to live their own lives, while also being willing to accompany them in their lives in a way that looks toward their good and not their harm. It means being honest, even when honesty is difficult or perhaps unwelcome. It doesn't mean trying to take control as if I were somehow more pleasing, better, closer to God than they.

We are all equal in love before God. Many of the aberrations of love arise from our failure to remember this. For example, we "love" another person beause we think she has all the attributes of beauty or goodness that we lack, but what we really want is to possess her and her good qualities for ourselves, to make up for our own deficiency. Or we "love" someone else because he seems weak and needy, enabling us to feel strong and rich. We want him to stay in that inferior position so that we can maintain the lie of our own superiority. Such "love" quickly becomes possessive, controlling, and destructive of both self and other. Genuine love sees the self and the beloved as fundamentally equal.

To love well, know yourself to be well loved. And know your neighbor as equally well loved—loved by God and therefore worthy of your love as well. In your neighbor, see your own partnership in love with God mirrored or, at the least, see God endeavoring to initiate such a partnership.

Since God's love for us is expressed in forgiveness, we can expect the same to be true of the love that derives from God's love. Every human being is loved and forgiven on exactly the same terms. This means that our love for our neighbor, as for ourselves, must often take the form of forgiveness, too.

Jesus was insistent on this point. We are to forgive as we are forgiven. We can ask for forgiveness, as in the Lord's Prayer, only insofar as we are willing to forgive. If we do not forgive, we cannot be forgiven (Matthew 6:12, 14-15).

Jesus' purpose here is not to set up rules by which you can earn or deserve forgiveness. It's too late for that. The very center of the good news is that God has forgiven us *before* we deserved it in any way.

The point, rather, is that the gift of forgiveness is offered equally to every human being. That is the only way God offers it. Therefore you cannot accept it for yourself while trying to deny it to someone else.

Often, this goes against the grain for us. And not only for us. It seemed to the authorities of Jesus' time that his message threatened to destroy religion and morality. It is certainly a very radical approach to the whole business of what human beings deserve from God.

Most of us can look around and see people whom we feel are less deserving than we—less deserving of respect, of success, of love, of esteem, of God's forgiveness. We may not want God to love those people the way God loves us. Perhaps it even cheapens God's love in our eyes.

But how else could God guarantee ongoing love for you? How else could God assure you that you will never, never fall below the reach of that love? If God cannot love the person who is worse than you, how can God love you the next time you fail? Are you perhaps already at the very lowest level to which God's love will stoop? Can you have any assurance that God's love for you will go on?

Here, then, is the choice we have: all are forgiven or none is forgiven. You may live in the world of the good news, where all people are forgiven, even those least worthy of it. Or you may live in a world where there is no such good news, a world where you must make your own way, a world where you can expect from God exactly what you deserve, no less, but also no more.

We'll talk later about what it means to live in that other world, the one where everyone gets exactly what she or he has deserved. For now, I want to talk more about what it means for us to live in the world of forgiveness—what it means for us to forgive one another.

*F*orgiveness, I think, is much misunderstood. Forgiveness is not a pretense, a fabrication, a lie about the past. It does not say, "Oh, that never happened," or "It didn't really make any difference," or "Everything is just as it was before." Forgiveness always begins by admitting the facts of the matter wherever there has been harm and hurt and wrongdoing.

Forgiveness does not mean telling lies about humanity, either—pretending that everyone is always straightforward, honest, kind, or good. Forgiveness isn't risk-free, of course, but it doesn't mean taking stupid and unnecessary risks with people who have shown themselves vicious or violent. It doesn't mean refusing to learn from the past or to take reasonable precautions for the future.

What forgiveness does mean is recognizing that we are not, at bottom, radically different from those who harm us—that we, too, have committed harm against others and may well do so again in the future, that those who injure us are human beings like us, that revenge will produce no particular good, for us any more than it will for them. Forgiveness, you might say, is a matter of acknowledging our fundamental kinship with those who have done us wrong.

This is not easy. When we have been wronged our first instinct, I think, is to dwell on the merits of our case. We make ourselves out to be even more innocent than we were. We stress the virtue of our status as victims of wrongdoing. Victimization, after all, constitutes a kind of merit, a claim on God's attention in its own right. If the harm was relatively trifling, we are apt to exaggerate the wrongdoing and paint those who hurt us as worse people than they are. If the harm was truly grave—or, at any rate, seemed so to us—we may begin to think of our enemies as scarcely belonging to the same human race as we do. (This is a fundamental step on the way to war and genocide and violent oppression of all kinds—the disposition to see your enemies as less than really human.) We may go on to plan revenge, justifying ourselves as merely seeking to right the wrong that had been done to us, to balance the account, to restore justice.

All of this is a very normal and human reaction to the wrongs done to us. Some of us go through this process very openly. Others conform outwardly to an ideal of generosity and forgiveness, while the process goes on inside them anyway. On the whole, the more open, honest process is preferable. After all, the good news is about truth, and real forgiveness can never be a form of lying.

Forgiveness begins when I understand that God loves and values the person next to me in just the same generous, unconditional way God loves me. Forgiveness means being will-ing that that should be so, accepting that the person who harmed me is still my brother or sister, recipient along with me of God's loving forgiveness, a part of my race and my family.

Forgiveness entails a certain letting go. It means letting go some of my sense of wounded innocence, remembering that I, too, am less than perfect. It means letting go my excessive devaluation of my enemy, admitting that she or he is still loved of God just as I am. It means letting go the desire for revenge and putting something else more compatible with the good news in its place.

What is this something else? As I've said, lies will not do. Forgiveness can be utterly hard-headed and clear-eyed. For-giving a child abuser does not mean that I will leave him alone with a child. Forgiving an embezzler does not mean that I will promptly reappoint her to a similar position of trust. Forgiveness does mean, however, that I can see those who have harmed me as more like myself than different and that I am prepared to build a future with them.

Human generosity can seldom, if ever, be as completely open as God's generosity; but God's generosity can still repre-sent the goal we hope to approximate. We move toward it when we refuse to write those who have wronged us off. We move toward it when we aim, with hope, at building a com-mon future rather than merely inflicting retribution.

The highest virtue, for Christians, is not justice, but love. Love means holding a door open, wherever possible, to the future. If your enemy will not go through it with you, hold it open anyway. Perhaps your enemy will change.

According to Matthew, Jesus held that the double commandment of love—love for God and equal love for self and neighbor—was fundamental. So fundamental, in fact, that all other moral law depends entirely on it for its authority. "On these two commandments," he says, "depend all the law and the prophets" (Matthew 22:40).

Paul said the same thing in another way. He held that the commandments were "summed up in this statement: You shall love your neighbor as yourself. Love works no harm to the neighbor. So love is the fullness of the law" (Romans 13:9-10).

John put it in yet another way: "God is love, and the person who remains in love remains in God and God in him" (1 John 4:16).

There is nothing on a par with love. No other principle of conduct or set of commandments modifies it, replaces it under certain circumstances, or has an authority independent of it.

This is a very important point. Christians have not always grasped its significance. Jesus felt quite free to reject and revise portions of the moral law that prevailed in his world. This law was, basically, the scriptural Law of Moses, the first five books of the Bible. Despite its authoritative status, both as Scripture and as the law of the Jewish nation in his time, he freely altered it, corrected it, reinterpreted it, rejected parts of it, pitted one part against another, broke it himself, and justified his followers in breaking it.

He even violated some of the Ten Commandments. He rejected his mother and the rest of his family and replaced them with his followers as his true family (Mark 3:31-35). He broke the law of the Sabbath by healing on it, even in non-emergency situations (see Mark 3:1-6; John 9). He defended his disciples when they violated the Sabbath by plucking grain (Mark 2:23-28).

Paul, like Jesus, set large parts of the Law of Moses aside. He championed the right of Gentiles to become Christians without first converting to Judaism. In the process, he exposed Jewish Christians who were in mixed congregations to the danger that they could no longer keep the purity laws that are such a prominent part of the Law of Moses. That's why he wrote that "love is the fullness of the law." Paul told the Christians at Rome: if you are loving your neighbor, you're keeping all the law there is. You can let go your anxieties about keeping the letter of the law, even about something as important to you as the laws of purity.

Love is a difficult law to interpret and to keep. For one thing, it is a very high standard. It is hard to love oneself well, honestly, and authentically; it is hard to love one's neighbor equally. Sometimes there are hard choices to be made among the objects of love. Sometimes we aren't rich enough to do it all. The idea that loving is enough can actually be fairly daunting.

Love is also a hard law to keep because it's relatively abstract. We don't always find it easy to determine what the loving thing is in a given situation. Our passions can cloud our reason. We can confuse other kinds of love—erotic love, for example—with the kind that Jesus and Paul were talking about. Or we can use the world "love" to manipulate people or to camouflage other motives.

There is always a great need for discernment, for discovering what really motivates us, or when we are talking one way and acting another. If we try to do this alone, it's fairly easy for us to fool ourselves. We need partners in discernment, particularly for the big decisions in our lives—people who share the good news and can help us interpret what love is asking of us.

Still, the relative "vagueness" of the principle of love remains—and will always remain—scary. You won't always be completely sure whether you've done what was right or whether you've done what was wrong. You have to continue exploring, hoping to understand yourself, your neighbor, and the meaning of love itself better.

This is not a bad thing. In fact, it's a very appropriate way for human beings to live. We are finite creatures who keep learning as we go. We cannot expect to know everything in advance. If a person doesn't know more about the complexities of life and love at the age of sixty than at twenty, that person has been wasting his or her life.

Still, we find the element of uncertainty alarming—particularly if we belong to the school of thought that wants clear and definite rules so that we can follow them and work our way into God's favor. As a result, there are always some Christians who want to turn away from love and replace it with something more concrete and unvarying. They think that Jesus and Paul were wrong, or that they cannot really have meant what they said. They think that there is more to the law than love, and that Christian morality has to include a great many specific rules of behavior. They have tried to remedy this "defect" by making lists of rules. Some Christians have even brought purity rules back in, some of them borrowed from the Law of Moses and others invented by Christians themselves.

"Yes," they say, "you are to love God and your neighbor, and maybe even yourself. But if you want to keep God's law, you must also go to church, receive communion a certain number of times in the year, be 'pure' in thought and deed, obey those in authority, maintain the standards of your community, be respectable, and hide those faults you can't get rid of."

But, ultimately, this approach turns Christianity into something not unlike the religion Jesus and Paul were attacking and undermining. That can't possibly be right. Jesus and Paul *did* mean what they said. They did not promise that living by the principle of love would be easy; they only said that it was right. It is right because it flows directly from the good news itself. If we accept God's love for us, we have to love one another.

The ordinary rules of human society, secular or religious, can give us some help here. They give us a general notion of what kind of behavior usually expresses respect for others and for oneself in a given place and time. If we find ourselves on the verge of violating the ordinary rules, we should probably think carefully about what we're really trying to accomplish. If we're convinced that we ought to violate them for the sake of conscience (that is, for the sake of love), we should take counsel with others and listen carefully to what they have to say. We should make revolutionary decisions with caution.

Still, for those who have received the good news, the rules of the church or of the society in which we live are only tentative authorities. We don't recognize them as having ultimate status.

The world at large—and the church along with it—has sanctioned all kinds of things that the principle of love cannot tolerate. Slavery, racism, the oppression of women and of the poor, homophobia—all these are ways of treating other human beings as if they were less human than we are. They are all violations of the principle of love. Yet, there are times when the most respectable people practice such things and churches contrive to live with them—sometimes even to advocate them and defend them on the grounds of principles other than love. People who have heard the good news should be resisting such inhumanities, not acquiescing in them.

The good news offers only one principle for interaction among human beings. That principle is the equal love of self and neighbor. Every action is good insofar as it conforms to it and bad insofar as it doesn't. It is the principle that must guide both our private and, wherever possible, our public lives if we wish to be people who live out of the good news.

Sometimes the early Christian writers seem to have been little concerned about the public sphere. In their day, most people were mere subjects of one empire or another, with little say about how they were governed. In our time, many of us, if not all, are citizens, so we have a much greater say. The principle of love, then, should be animating not only our behavior as individuals, but our vision of what is possible within our communities and even among nations.

To move toward a world in which the principle of love is taken seriously will still be a long and difficult process, but it should be possible now in ways that it has not been in the past. We have had ample evidence in the past century of the terrible wrongs worked by ethnic and racial hatreds, by the contempt of one class for another, or by sexual arrogance. The world will not be safe for any of us until it is safe for us all. However difficult the principle of love, and however demanding and hard at times to define, love is the only moral principle that opens a door to the future. When I truly believe that I am as human as you and you are as human as I, that God loves us indistinguishably, I shall begin building a different kind of world.

A lawyer once asked Jesus precisely how far the principle of love had to extend. Exactly who was the neighbor he was supposed to love as himself?

Jesus answered with a story about a Jewish man who was mugged and left for dead on the road to Jericho (Luke 10:29-37). A priest of the Jerusalem Temple came by but kept his distance. He may have feared that the man was dead and that touching the corpse would pollute him and leave him unable to perform his services in the Temple. Later, a levite from the Temple passed by and avoided the man, perhaps for the same reason. Finally, a Samaritan came along, a hereditary enemy of the Jews, a man who might have been expected to pass by as well. Yet, he picked the man up, gave him first aid, loaded him on his donkey, took him to an inn, cared for him, and, when he left, paid the innkeeper to go on taking care of him as long as necessary.

"Who," Jesus asked the lawyer, "do you think turned out to be neighbor to the man who got mugged?" "The one who behaved kindly toward him," said the lawyer.

Give as you have been given to. Learn your generosity from the generosity you have received—from God's generosity, yes, but also from *any* act of generosity, including the generosity of enemies, of people you might otherwise treat with contempt, of outcasts, of police officers, of prostitutes, of superiors and of inferiors, of scoundrels, and also of friends, of family, of those like you in age or race or sex or sexual orientation, of benefactors, of saints. . . . The point is not the goodness or badness of the other, but the willingness to reach across what separates us and to treat one another as human beings loved by God.

*L*ove yourself and your neighbor alike. Do it with reasonable caution. Jesus advises his followers to be "gentle as doves," but also "wise as serpents" (Matthew 10:16). The good news is not a summons to suicidal silliness. But remember that your neighbor, even at the worst, is fundamentally like you—in the same position before God as you are. We are all in that position together—forgiven, loved, and summoned to love. If we want to live into the future, we shall have to risk doing it together.

6

Refusing Good News

God's love and forgiveness have no conditions on them. They are given you whether you accept them or reject them. God leaves you free, but doesn't withdraw the offered gift.

Still, it makes a real difference whether you say "yes" or "no." Or, more precisely, whether you are *beginning* to say "yes" or "no," for no one, I think, succeeds in saying the whole "yes" or "no" once for all at the beginning. We answer with our whole lives, not with a single moment of them.

Saying "yes" to God's gift brings you into partnership in love with God. It gives you a new place to stand, a new reason to love yourself, and a new way to love the creation of which you are a part and God's other loved and forgiven people. It gives you a new world to live in and new ways of living in it. This "yes" is a very powerful word.

Saying "no" is also powerful. Our "no" also makes a certain kind of world for us to live in and mandates a certain kind of behavior toward ourselves and one another.

If we say "no" to God's forgiveness, we are saying that we want some other kind of relationship with God and the world—probably a relation based on what we deserve rather than what God freely gives.

But wait a moment. Isn't it possible that a person who says "no" to the good news is really saying "no" to God as such, doesn't want any relation with God, and doesn't even believe that God exists? Certainly there are many people who reject the idea of God and, in that sense, are uninterested in a relationship with God. They find the whole notion, in fact, meaningless and unthinkable.

Yet, no one, I think, actually evades the reality of God. No one succeeds in ignoring it altogether. The word "God" means many things, but at the very least it is a way of talking about, alluding to, and pointing toward our own finitude.

Reality is much bigger than we are. It sets limits for us at every turn: we are people of a particular place and time, a particular class, a particular language, a particular education, people who enjoy certain successes and suffer certain failures, people who are well or sick, people with particular family and friends, enemies and acquaintances and associates. Eventually, we will each meet a final boundary to our world in the form of death.

No human being can see clearly across these limits. We have little or no power over the reality beyond them. If religious people speak of that reality as "God," that doesn't mean they know in detail the shape of that reality. They are only gesturing toward it and saying, "It seems more like this than that."

God is object of faith, not knowledge. God is glimpsed, hinted at, guessed at, gestured toward. God contains us, limits us, defines us. God knows us; we don't yet really know God (1 Corinthians 13:12).

When we talk about God, then, we are talking about the reality that limits and defines us. That such a reality exists is undeniable. Whatever you choose to call it, you will run up against it. You will have to think about it and imagine it and deal with it and live in the midst of it.

And how will you live in the midst of it? I think there are two possible choices. You can live as someone who is loved without regard to your deserving it, or you can live as someone who wants to have exactly what you believe you have deserved.

Perhaps there is a third choice, too, and that is to live as if the greater reality cared nothing about you one way or another, as if there is no meaning in your life other than what you yourself can create. Perhaps there is this third choice, although I have not known anyone who really managed to live by it.

Most of us assume life has some kind of integrated meaning. And most of us would like to live not by God's generosity nor by anyone else's, but by what we have deserved. Most of us at least give it a try at some point in our lives.

When Jesus told the story about the wastrel son who absconded with "his" share of the family fortune and then came home penniless, he put in another part that I left out when I retold the story above. This other part is about the elder brother, who was a hard-working, dutiful, responsible man who was probably quite admirable in many ways.

This older brother heard that his father had thrown a party to welcome the bad son back home. He got very angry about it and refused to go into the house and join the celebration. Instead, he stood outside. He stood on his own worth. He was outraged that his younger brother was being rewarded after all his bad behavior.

The father went out to the older son with every show of respect and honor and affection, just as he had gone out to meet the younger one. He wanted to bring him inside. But the older son was having none of it. He made an angry speech about how deserving he himself was and how little his father had done to recognize and repay that. The father, in turn, urged on him a kind of generosity: "Your brother is back from the dead. We should celebrate."

We don't know how the righteous brother responded. Did he stay outside, sulking, licking his wounds, complaining about a world that didn't take his merits seriously? Or did he decide to join the celebration of his brother's safe return?

It's easy to sympathize with the elder brother. The father's behavior was more generous than it was just. The older son *was* a more responsible, loyal, deserving person than the younger. Yet, by refusing the good news of his father's forgiving love, by insisting that his own merits be rewarded first, he succeeded only in cutting himself out of a party.

The question, finally, is not, "Which brother was in the right?" The question is, "What is the world like? Which way does God really behave? Which is the better description of reality?"

It may seem harmless enough to insist on having our merits rewarded. It may even seem like a good idea, since justice is, on the whole, a good thing among human beings. Without it, society loses its moral claim and its stability. Yet, eventually, the idea of justice reaches a limit—for example, in situations like Ireland or the Near East, where everyone has a legitimate complaint against everyone else. Justice, then, is a very good thing in itself, but it doesn't hold any final answers. Luke tells us that a man once came to Jesus asking for help in getting his inheritance from his brother. Maybe his elder brother, who was in charge, was trying to keep the family property together in his own hands. Jesus, despite his basic sympathy with the underdog, ran the man off, saying, "Who made me a judge and a divider over you?" (Luke 12:14).

Under certain circumstances, justice has to give way to something more powerful and more life-giving—generosity, forgiveness, love. The alternative—what you would get if you clung to justice alone—is not a well-ordered, decent, well-behaved world, but something that ultimately turns out to be ugly and destructive.

Think again of the older brother in the parable. He is not, finally, an appealing character. By taking his stand on his own goodness, he becomes sour, mean, unforgiving—a burden both to himself and to the rest of the family.

This is what happens if we refuse the world of the good news and choose, instead, to live in a world where we have to endear ourselves to God or make claims on God based on our own goodness. We reject being loved by God as too small a thing, and seek instead to deserve well of God. We reject God's initiative, God's determination to love us unconditionally, in season and out of season, and replace it with an initiative of our own: we propose to control or compel God's love of us by making ourselves so worthy of it that God cannot refuse.

But, for better or worse, the world doesn't work that way. Everyday experience confounds this notion. It is impossible to pretend for long that good comes only to the deserving, that the world always treats the pious well, that God's care is confined to those who deserve it. As Jesus says, "God makes his sun rise on evil people and on good and rains on just people and on unjust" (Matthew 5:45). This world in which we live doesn't operate on any simple, straightforward merit system.

Since the notion that we can compel God's love by deserving it doesn't square with reality, to live by this notion means we have to lie. And to protect our lie we have to grow mean and narrow, despising other people and dealing harshly with ourselves.

There is no human behavior that Jesus opposed more absolutely than this kind of lying. "The devil," he says, "is a liar" (John 8:44). He saves his angriest words for the hypocrisy of the religious authorities of his day. "Hypocrites" is his word for them. "Do and keep all they tell you," he tells his followers, "but don't do as they do" (Matthew 23:3). Their *idea* of what is good is all right, but they themselves only pretend to practice it.

It is hard for us, at times, to think of hypocrisy as a fundamental evil. We've grown to accept it as a normal part of respectable existence—maybe even a necessary part. As the proverb has it, "Hypocrisy is the tribute vice pays to virtue." Surely, we may think, there are many things worse than hypocrisy.

Not so, according to Jesus. For Jesus, the good news is not about being respectable, nor is it about being or appearing to be righteous or pious. The good news is about being loved and forgiven. If you want to deal with reality, he says, this is what you must deal with.

If, on the other hand, you want to pretend that reality is about getting what you deserve, you will have to lie endlessly. You must think well of yourself so that you will feel you deserve something of God. You must think ill of your neighbors, so that you can at least feel more deserving than they. You must think well of the successful, since they must surely have deserved their success. You must think ill of all who have failed or suffered, since they, too, must be getting what they deserve. You must assume that the manners and mores of the successful and the respectable are what pleases God; you must assume that those of the poor displease God.

All of this is a lie, and it gives rise to deep-rooted evil in those who believe it. The meanness and hardness of the older brother in the parable was no accident. It was a direct result of his preoccupation with his own goodness.

Jesus repeatedly faced such attitudes from members of the religious elite of his own day. At one point, he responded to them with the one truly absolute and sweeping condemnation he ever uttered against anyone (Matthew 12:22-32; Mark 3:20-30).

He had been exorcising people who were possessed by demons—surely as clearcut and unalloyed a demonstration of God's generosity as one could hope to encounter in the first-century world. The religious authorities, however, claimed that his act of healing was a fake. They said Jesus was really serving the demonic powers that he claimed to be casting out.

Jesus rejects their charge. He notes that they never question the exorcisms their own partisans perform. Their accusation is animated not by anything amiss in Jesus' work, but entirely by their fear of his growing influence and their unwillingness to think that God could be working through someone who was not a part of their group.

Finally, Jesus charges the authorities with committing the one sin that is beyond all forgiveness: "Amen, amen, I tell you that all things will be forgiven the children of humanity—all the sins and the blasphemies that they commit. But whoever blasphemes against the Holy Spirit has no forgiveness ever, but is liable for an eternal sin." He said this, Mark tells us, because, when he was exorcising, they had said, "He has an unclean spirit."

What exactly was this unforgivable sin that the religious authorities committed (and which they—or we—are always in danger of committing)? It was the sin of calling good evil in order to protect your own moral and religious superiority.

The authorities did not want to take Jesus seriously because he challenged their sense of themselves as deserving God's particular favor. And so they looked at the good he did and called it evil, so that they could go on claiming that they alone were God's chosen.

This is where we wind up when we want to live by our own deserving rather than by God's forgiving love. We do not wind up being better than others, but worse. We wind up telling massive lies so that we can always feel assured that we are better, more lovable, and more loved than anyone else. Eventually, we wind up caught in our own lies—so persuaded by them that we begin to see good as evil, Holy Spirit as unclean spirit, God's love as demonic, God's forgiveness as immoral, ourselves as the last bastion of goodness. We are locked into a sin that does not admit of its own forgiveness.

Why, after all, is this sin unforgivable? Because God is unwilling to forgive it? Hardly. Why should God's generosity stop here? It is unforgivable because, once we are locked into it, fully committed to it, immersed in it, losing sight of anything other than our own righteousness, we cannot let ourselves accept forgiveness. To accept forgiveness would be to admit that we have something for which we need to be forgiven. It would put us on a level with sinners. It would deprive of us of our assurance that, unlike them, we deserve something from God.

Even if we don't imagine ourselves as perfect, we will at least take refuge in the thought that we are better than the people around us. We'll want God to validate and reward our deservingness. We won't accept anything else. If all God wants to do is forgive, we find we would rather do without.

At this point, we have become our own gods. Or rather, our righteousness has become our god. We have fallen in love with our own goodness, and this is the one other love that God will not accept in us.

From the time when God wooed Israel at Sinai, God insisted that there be no other gods or idols (Exodus 20:3-6). There is only the one God, who loves us no matter what. There is no other real god. To love another god means to love a lie.

We are very energetic and creative in the lies we invent. We make gods out of strength, beauty, riches, success, family, enjoyment, morality, piety—anything a person can possibly value. We love them as if they were the ultimate reality. Since they are not, they eventually leave us in the lurch, either failing to give us the satisfaction we expected or abandoning us altogether.

We also like to make idols—images of gods that we can keep close to us, where we hope to influence and control them and compel them to give us what we want. We make idols out of our jobs, and by excessive labor or questionable compromises we hope to charm the god to grant us success. We make an idol out of sex, and by devoting our every attention to the pursuit of it we hope to compel the god to grant us love. We make an idol out of domestic life, and by sacrificing ourselves and those around us we hope to make the god give us the perfect middle-class family.

We even make idols of the true God, and suppose we can make this God love us more by our piety and devotion to them. We sacrifice ourselves and others to the supposed demands of church or Bible in order to make these idols happy.

The result has been some bizarre violations of the good news. Over our long history, Christians have at times killed people for believing the wrong things, forced people to convert at sword's point, imprisoned people for violating the "sabbath," enslaved non-believers, made women keep silent and confine themselves to domestic work, encouraged the abuse of gay and lesbian people. And Christianity is not unique in this regard. All religions have in them this potential to be used in an idolatrous way.

But it is all completely useless as well as completely wrong. God cannot love you more. God already loves you completely. All the sacrifices of self and others that you make in this way are completely misdirected and pointless.

As long as we avoid idolatry, the Christian religion can be a way of celebrating and sharing the good news. The church can be a community of discernment where we hear the good news in ways that illuminate our own lives and share with others in figuring out how better to conform our lives to it.

There is nothing intrinsically wrong with religion; and I'll have more to say, later on, about the ways we can put church and Scripture to proper use. Idolatry, however, even the most religious idolatry in the world, is an unmitigated evil. It is evil because it is a lie. It offers an illusion of control over gods that, even if you can control them, are ultimately no gods at all. Or it promises control over the one God, who cannot be controlled and whom we have no need to control.

The final end of hypocrisy is absolute death. Hypocrisy means imagining yourself beyond all need of God's love—and thus, in a certain sense, beyond all reach of it. The fruit of hypocrisy is a self-righteous isolation, continually walling itself in more and more deeply to preserve itself from the impure contagion of the wicked and to reassure itself of its own superiority.

The one possible remedy against this death is the good news that God still loves. Even in your hypocrisy, God loves. God is only waiting for you to say "yes" to God's love instead of your own goodness.

*J*esus told a story about a man who had a vineyard (Matthew 20:1-16). He went to the marketplace early in the day and hired day-laborers at the standard wage and sent them to work in his vineyard. He went back a few hours later and hired more and sent them out, promising to pay them "whatever's right." He did the same thing twice more during the day. Then, when it was almost dark, he did it yet again.

At quitting time, the owner of the vineyard began to pay the laborers. He first called up the ones who had only worked for an hour—and paid them a full day's wage! The people who had worked all day were watching and thinking, "You watch—he'll have to pay us more." But when their turn came, he paid them the same amount.

The people who had worked all day got angry and complained. The owner replied, "Friend, I'm doing you no wrong. You're getting what we agreed on. I want to give to this last person just as I'm giving to you. Am I not allowed to do what I want with what belongs to me? Or are you jealous because I am good?"

The answer, often, is "yes." We get jealous when God is good to someone else, especially someone we see as less deserving than we are. If we get jealous enough, we may even decide to throw our own wages on the ground and walk off in anger. But it's our anger, not God's goodness, that is at fault.

God is not driving the righteous, the hard-working, the responsible away. God is welcoming them in right alongside their opposites. You have a secure place in God's love, whichever group you belong to. The question is, will you set your own claims aside long enough to accept it?

7

Good News and Heaven

The good news offers us a new world to live in. Not an unreal fantasy world to escape into, but a world that is more real, more enduring, more true than any other. Yet in many ways this promised world may seem radically removed, and radically different, from the everyday world we have known. We sense ourselves both as living in it now and as not yet living in it. If the promised world is to make sense in relation to our lived experience, we have to understand it as a transformation of our present world—a new world of which we are in the vanguard.

It is easy to misunderstand this idea. Christians have often presented the promised world as something essentially disconnected from the present or connected to it only incidentally. They treat this world, for example, as a struggle or contest and that world as the prize. Accordingly, they tell us to behave or feel or believe in a certain way here and now in order to receive the very different life of heaven as reward. Or they treat this life as a test to see who will deserve entry into that higher world, and they tell us to accept misery and meaninglessness in this world in order to enjoy the world to come. Either way, we have been told that this life is a time for duty or suffering, while the world to come is the time to see God face to face. The emphasis, often as not, has been on how unlike these two worlds are.

This is odd teaching to be coming from Christians. Christians decided definitively, in the second century of our era, that we believe in a God who is creator of this present world, not just of the world to come. Did God create this world, rejoice in it, and praise it merely in order to make it a hurdle on the way to salvation? Did our human turning away from God have such corrosive force that this world became altogether displeasing in God's sight?

Genesis tells a story which at first suggests that it might be so. In the days of Noah, the story goes, God found human behavior so detestable that he decided to destroy the world with a flood and start over again. Yet, after the flood, God decided that he had acted hastily and vowed never to do the same again (Genesis 6:11-9:17). God reaffirmed that the world is good and that God is committed to sustaining and working within it.

If the same God creates both this world and the world to come, the two cannot be altogether unlike each other. In fact, the reality is even more complex than that. The two worlds actually interpenetrate in our present lives. Those who have heard and received the good news are now living in two worlds at once. They are residents here, residing in the same world we have known all along, but their citizenship lies elsewhere—in the age to come, in "heaven," to use the traditional term.

What is heaven? Heaven is a life characterized by peace, love, fulfillment. But, no, that may misrepresent heaven by making it sound static and bland. Let me put the same thing another way: heaven is a life characterized by triumph, by delight, by a happy dialectic between desire, opportunity, and achievement. Heaven is new life, life constantly renewed in the power and love of God. Heaven is a world characterized by human affection, friendship, and intimacy, by beauty that speaks to all the senses, by a richness that does not grow wearisome with time. One image for it is the Peaceable Kingdom, where all people and animals live peaceably side by side (Isaiah 11:1-10). Another image is that of a cosmic picnic with a never-failing supply of good food and drink (Isaiah 25:6-9), while still another is that of a splendid city, the heavenly Jerusalem, with a beautiful river flowing through it and a garden in its midst (Revelation 21:9-22:5).

This is the kind of life that would make the highest sense of our humanity. We are not pure spirit, attuned to timeless contemplation. We are not pure body, satisfied with bare

73

sensation. We are complex, composite beings, constantly in motion, testing boundaries, learning from the things and people we encounter, reflecting, discovering, becoming new, losing hold of things we thought were secure, reaching out for things whose existence we had not imagined a few months before, fearing, loving, helping, being helped, giving and receiving a host of goods. We are befriended and befriending, loved and loving. We are enlightened and transformed by beauty, fulfilled and made transparent by delight. No world that cannot accommodate such complexity is a true home for human beings.

Our present world accommodates us fitfully—enough for us to see our potential, but seldom enough for us to achieve the greater part of it. Even so, this world in which we live gives us the opportunity to begin living the life of the world to come here and now. You do not have to wait for the end of time or the resurrection of all the dead to begin living as citizens of heaven. You begin here and now, learning step by step how to let God's forgiving love permeate your life and make of you not only a citizen of the world to come, but a door, a path, an opening into it.

The present age won't always be friendly to this project. It did, after all, crucify Jesus and martyr a good many of his early followers. Yet, the triumph of heaven can come to expression in human lives even in a sometimes hostile world. It is a triumph of forgiveness over revenge, of generosity over greed, of love over hate, of hope over fear, of integrity and truth over lying and hypocrisy.

By just these means, people who have received the good news become gates through which the life of the age to come begins to penetrate this present age. As we are transformed, we press against the sometimes narrow confines and defensive limits of this age.

The benefit is not only to those who get something out of our generosity and hope, our love and integrity. We also benefit, ourselves, by the increasing honesty and unity of our lives. We are free to surrender illusions of our own goodness, of superiority to our neighbors, of our own ultimate power and righteousness and deservingness. We are free to live as ordinary human beings who have received extraordinary gifts and now live from the riches of these gifts.

There is no simple formula for such a life. There can't be. No unambiguous set of rules, followed by rote, will ever make a person honest or simple or good. What is right at one place and time can be wrong at another. What is common to the life of heaven, as lived throughout this world by its citizens, is not a set of rules, but the fact that it is animated by the good news, received in faith, hope, and love and expressed in action. Work out how to live these things in your particular, unique life and you are beginning to live the life of heaven, even if the country where you find yourself seems an alien one.

The alternative to heaven is living the life of hell. Sometimes hell seems more available and stronger here and now than heaven. Ultimately, however, it is weaker. Love builds—both for the lover and for the beloved. Hatred destroys the hater even more surely than the object of hatred. Truth, however painful it sometimes is, opens the door to life and growth.

Hypocrisy sucks out the souls of those who practice it and leaves them empty, dry, resentful husks.

Still, there is a great temptation to choose the life of hell in this world. The temptation is this: hell appears to give you more power against others and more control over yourself. The gods of hell have good public relations agents and are easy to market. They are free to make all kinds of false promises. The god of Career promises that, if you sacrifice diligently for many years, you will be rich and secure and happy. The god of Nation promises that, if you pile up arms and seal your borders and exclude those different from you, you will be invulnerable. The god of Pleasure promises that you will need nothing else ever. The god of Family promises that, for a certain price in personal freedom, you will be guaranteed warmth and affection for life. The god of Self-assurance promises that, if you cultivate your own divinity with appropriate meditations and exercises, you can triumph over any opposition whatever. The god of Respectability promises that, if you curb yourself and make yourself just like everyone else, no unexpected harm can ever come to you.

All these promises—and the thousand others like them—have plausibility. They are not absolute lies. They begin with the good things of this creation, such as work and wealth and pleasure, family and community and self—things that are genuinely good and genuinely desirable. Yet there is a subtle twist in the promises they make.

The promises move from "These things are good; enjoy them" to "These things are supreme; serve them." By serving them, we hope to share their supremacy; we hope, absurdly enough, to gain control of our own lives. We think we can use work or nation or family or positive attitudes or whatever as tools to gain security for ourselves; instead, we are in danger of becoming their tools.

To put a simple label on it, the life of hell is *idolatry*. Idolatry makes us subservient to whatever lesser values we have chosen to worship. So far from giving us life, it takes life away. It keeps us busy in its own service. It gives us rewards the way slot machines do—just enough to keep us interested, never enough to cost the casino anything.

Thus your work becomes not a means to exist or a contribution to the world, but the goal of your life. Your family becomes not a group of people with whom you share a history, but the justification of your own existence. You may play their servant, trying to control by manipulation, or their master, trapped in the struggle to rule by decree; in either case, without them you cease to exist. Your nation ceases to be the arena in which you cooperate with others for justice and the general welfare and becomes a Moloch that devours the lives of the young, the marginal, the stranger. Your self-confidence ceases to be a tool and becomes something you spend your life to sustain.

*I*dolatry represents not only a lie about power, but a drastic oversimplification of human existence. No human being exists simply for one purpose. We exist, as Scripture says, in God's image. That means we are able to create, to interact with, and to love many things and people. On our own finite scale, we are like God, creating our own worlds. They should be rich and varied, clear and beautiful.

Our great difference from God, in this respect, is that we never begin with a blank slate; we cannot start from scratch. Our worlds will never be exclusively ours, for they must take account of the other worlds that border on them and interpenetrate them. Therefore, our human existence—if it is being lived realistically and honestly—must always be a kind of conversation. We make our contribution to it, and we must pay attention also to the contributions of others: of God, of the created order, of our fellow human beings.

This is the life of heaven—a conversation that is long, rich, active, ongoing, one that is never boring (unless I detach myself from it) or wasted or stupid or pointless. It is a conversation not only of minds, but of souls and bodies as well. We converse not only through thoughts and words, but through feelings and actions. Everything we do is a part of this conversation, as much so as everything we say. Perhaps more so, since what we do may involve us more fully than our words.

No one can live fully as a human being without recognizing this reality. No human being is an "unmoved mover." No human being can shape his or her world exactly to personal specification. To be human means to be part of the human race, to be involved in its enormous, ongoing conversation with itself and its world. We have received our humanness from others. We, in turn, are helping shape the humanness of those around us. Either you are a part of this process or you are not a human being.

You may never fully realize the life of heaven in the here and now, but you can make a beginning. You can begin to abandon hell. You can accept the therapy of truth and begin to recover from addiction to lies—the lies that have kept you subject to your idols. You can choose the full-bodied (if sometimes risky) life of integrity over the shadowy (and ultimately lethal) existence of hypocrisy. You can claim the citizenship of heaven now by every action that flows out of the good news. And when you claim it, it is yours.

And is there more? Is there really a place named heaven where all this comes to fulfillment? If God is powerful enough to have created this world, God is powerful enough to create the age to come. If God is creative and surprising enough to initiate the good news, God is creative and surprising enough to bring it to fruition.

For now, we are in a situation where we are free to respond or not, as we wish. There is a risk in exercising your heavenly citizenship—the risk that the good news may be wrong after all, the risk that this world either makes no sense, finally, or is under the control of evil, hatred, and anger. Yet the risk is smaller than it may seem. Those who embrace the good news in integrity, with faith, hope, and love, discover that life is at work in them, that they are being freed from old slaveries, that the future is becoming more open, not less. The good news encourages and illuminates and sustains a life of courage and generosity. For now, that may be enough to know. The ultimate heaven can take care of itself.

Jesus told a story about the last judgment (Matthew 25:31-46). He said that the final judge would be seated on the bench and would gather all the people of the world before him. There he would divide them into two groups, like a shepherd separating sheep from goats in the evening after they have grazed all day together, putting the sheep on the right and the goats on the left. Then the judge will say to the ones on the right, "You are blessed. You are citizens of heaven. You have taken care of me when I was needy—hungry, sick, in prison, naked." They all reply, "Oh, but you're mistaken. When did we do that?" "You did it whenever you did such a kindness to anyone at all."

And to the ones on the left, the judge says, "You belong in hell. You never did me any kindness when I was needy—no food, no visit, no clothes." They all say, "Oh, but you're mistaken. When did we ever fail to do that?" "You did it whenever you failed to show kindness to anyone else."

It is a terrifying story, in one way. Is there anyone who has not at some time ignored the need of another? In another way, it has a note of promise about it. The promise is not that you can earn your way into the kingdom of heaven. The promise is that you can begin living there now. Even a cup of water given to the thirsty is heaven breaking through into the here and now. Heaven is as much a possibility in your life now as hell.

The judge is not saying, "You passed an arbitrary test; now you can go to heaven and enjoy your reward." The judge is not saying, "You failed an arbitrary test; now you must go to hell and suffer your punishment." The judge is saying, "You are a citizen of heaven. Heaven is at work in you. Enjoy the freedom of your true country." Or, "You don't seem to have claimed your citizenship. You would not be at home here."

At this point, Jesus' image of sending one group of people to heaven and the other to hell has taken us as far as it can go. To insist that it go further would be misleading. Hell is not merely a place to which the wicked will one day be sent, but the place where the liars, the cruel, and the cynical are living right now. Or, looked at another way, hell is the power living in them. Those who belong to hell take their hell with them wherever they go. You cannot enter heaven without heaven entering you.

Even God cannot admit you to heaven unless you claim your citizenship there. If a person filled with hell could be "in" heaven, it would only be hell for that person. Conversely, claiming your citizenship brings with it the opportunity to belong to heaven right now. Therefore we are summoned to claim our citizenship now, to begin living as citizens of heaven now, even if that means accepting that we may have to be resident aliens in a world where hell is a real possibility, too. However vulnerable the life of faith, hope, and love may sometimes seem, it is the only human existence that truly builds toward the future, the only one that can survive in the long run.

8

Good News, God, and Jesus

The people who first heard the good news of Jesus seem to have begun feeling, early on, that Jesus did more than relay that news, as a messenger might. Instead, he embodied it; he *was* the good news.

The good news came out in his actions as well as his words: in the way he accepted all who came to him, the way he touched the impure without fear, the way he shared meals with ordinary folk who had no great claim to piety or respectability, the way he warned the devout about the dangers of their hypocrisy, the way he brought all sorts and conditions of people together in his inner circle, the way he welcomed women into that inner circle, the way he stuck with his message against opposition, the way he faced death with integrity. Jesus embodied what he taught.

More than that, he embodied it as if God were in him, making this offer of loving forgiveness directly to humanity. Jesus acted as if God's power were present in his own work: he forgave sins, exorcised demons, healed the sick, cleansed lepers, raised the dead, taught a new way of being faithful and loving in the world, created a new community among his followers.

People felt that, in meeting Jesus, they had not only heard the good news, but had met God proclaiming the good news.

This is difficult to talk about clearly. We have no direct and straightforward language, really, for speaking about God. Mostly, we have to rely on metaphors. We can do little more than gesture toward God and describe how we feel in God's presence. All the Christian language about God being in Jesus should be understood in this way, as an effort to express the ungraspable. Sometimes theological language sounds quite precise—but the precision is metaphorical.

Over a period of centuries, Christian doctrine worked out what it means to say that Jesus is "incarnate God." Christians say that Jesus is "truly God and truly human"—fully and authentically God and fully and authentically a real human being. If this is impossible to imagine, that's all right. The doctrine was never meant to explain anything; only to point toward a truth that, like all truth about God, remains to some degree permanently beyond the grasp of human language and understanding. The main thing, still, is that original sense people had—the sense of encountering God in Jesus, of being assured that the good news in Jesus is seriously meant *by* God *for* you.

Jesus' humanity is every bit as important, theologically, as his divinity. It means that God is truly concerned with us and truly available to us in the here and now. God is present not only through the humanity of Jesus, but through all humanity in Jesus—your own humanity and that of your neighbor included.

Jesus' story about the Last Judgment, as we have seen, affirms this: the judge, seated on the bench, says to the condemned, "You never came to my help when I needed you." They answer, "We never knew you needed us." Jesus says, "Whenever *anybody* needed you, it was I."

Jesus' sufferings are ours, and ours are Jesus'. And the same is true of his triumph.

The gospels tell us that Jesus' crucifixion was not the final act in his story, but that God raised him from the dead into a new, larger, freer, unending life. This is not an ordinary miracle of the sort most of us witness at some time or other in our lives—a moment when the utterly improbable happens and restores the fabric of life as we commonly know it. This is an extraordinary moment. It tears the fabric of this world open and gives a glimpse of something else beyond.

The astonishing thing is to find that our humanity belongs there, in the world beyond, as well as here. Jesus does not shed his humanity in the resurrection, or turn from being human back into being God, or become something other than human, such as a disembodied spirit, a ghost, an angel. It is Jesus the human being that walks through the rent made in reality by his death and resurrection—and so becomes "the pioneer, the trailblazer, of our well-being" (Hebrews 2:10).

Jesus' resurrection will be our resurrection, too—the ultimate triumph of the good news. The resurrection is not an isolated event of the past, but the first installment, the down payment of a world-transforming process, one that Christian tradition speaks of as "the general resurrection" of all the dead, leading into the life of the world to come. Again we are speaking in metaphorical language. Who has ever seen this or can have any direct knowledge of it? But this metaphor gestures toward a profound truth that we can find at work already in this life.

We don't wait for the general resurrection before we begin living the life of the age to come. We are citizens of that age here and now. And to live as citizens of the age to come, even here and now, however risky it may be, is also the key to life and growth. However demanding they are, the good news and its principles of love do not cost more than they give. Just the reverse, they produce a new integrity, coherence, and vitality in our existence. They bring good out of evil, peace out of anger, new life out of apparent defeat and disaster.

As we begin to experience the power of that life in us here and now, the resurrection of Jesus (and our own with it) ceases to be incredible. Quite the contrary, it fits in with our own present experience even while it also goes far beyond it. The power that we find already transforming us right now is great enough to transform the world.

God is in Jesus, living out the good news. We are in Jesus, living out the good news.

Jesus is both God and human being. Being God, he is eternally present; he is the power that shapes and upholds this world. Being human, Jesus belonged, like all human beings, to a particular community and place and time—in his case, the Jewish people of Roman Palestine in the first century of our era.

The message Jesus preached was originally directed to people of his own community, place, and time. Since then, it has spread throughout the world and assumed different forms so that it could still be good news even to people quite different from Jesus' original audience. Jesus prepared his followers for this transformation by giving them the gift of the Holy Spirit.

Who or what is the Spirit? Jesus knew the Spirit under Hebrew and Aramaic names (*ruah*, *ruha*) which happen to be of feminine gender. Accordingly, I'll refer to the Spirit here as "she." It's important to remember, however, that such language, like the "he" we often use with reference to God, is metaphorical. Our language doesn't describe the Spirit or any other divine substance. It can't, because they are beyond our grasp. It only gestures toward them.

The ancient words for Spirit also mean "wind." And Jesus says that the Spirit is indeed like the wind. You don't know where the wind comes from or where it is going (John 3:8). Similarly, the work of the Spirit always has about it an element of elusiveness and surprise.

We cannot pin the Spirit down. It is difficult to contemplate her or speak about her in her own right. The Spirit doesn't stay in the same place or keep on doing only one and the same thing for ever. By virtue of the Spirit, Jesus' good news always contains the possibility of change and growth, of adaptation to new situations and addressing new audiences.

Jesus, being a real human being, is in some sense absent from us today. He belongs to another time and place. He is present in the good news and in the sacraments of the good news. But he is not with us in the same sense that he was with his first followers before the crucifixion. He isn't here to enjoy or endure the exact circumstances of our lives here and now, to live at a particular address, to be questioned or challenged, to respond to modern problems, to preach a sermon or sit down to supper with a group of our own religious outcasts.

Instead, Jesus has left the Spirit with us. She is indeed present: not at a particular address, not under human control, but in the same way the wind is present—free, powerful, often unexpected. Jesus promises that the Spirit will lead his followers in all truth. The Spirit takes what belongs to Jesus and proclaims it to us (John 16:13).

Jesus told his followers to rely on the guidance of the Spirit. Sometimes that has produced problems. After all, any one can *claim* the inspiration of the Spirit, but it's hard to test such claims, either to verify or to refute them.

One of Jesus' early followers urged people to test spiritual claims by the behavior of those making the claims. Do they respect others in the Christian community? Do they contribute to the well-being of the group? Does their behavior express love? (1 Corinthians 12-14)

Another early follower urged us to look for continuity with Jesus' own message. A spirit that teaches something other than love or refuses to acknowledge the importance of Jesus is not likely to be the same as Jesus' Spirit. (1 John 4)

If we remember these tests and apply them with love and respect for one another, we find that the Spirit makes Jesus' good news present among us in new and living ways. The Spirit keeps us from trying to fix the good news in a permanent, unchanging form—a process that can only fossilize it. She keeps reawakening us, instead, to the living reality of it and the way it reshapes our world and ourselves here and now.

God—the God who made us and loves us—was in Jesus proclaiming good news in word and in deed. In Jesus, God died with us. In Jesus, we have been raised with God.

And God continues to stir up new life in us through the Spirit, Jesus' gift to all. By trusting the Spirit's guidance, in continuity with Jesus' work and words and in common with one another, we can greet, with surprise and joy, the good news in our own time and place, however different from that of Jesus.

9

Good News and the Bible

As Jesus says, it is the Spirit that gives life (John 6:63). The Spirit is free to go anywhere and to respond in new ways to new situations. The Spirit enables the good news to go on being *news*, even when it is centuries old.

Therefore, the Spirit stands in a certain tension with all fixed and predictable religious forms. Fixed forms are valuable because they can remind us of God's love. But they cannot take the place of the Spirit. The Spirit is the living, moving, surprising, innovative quality of the good news that enables it to be good news for you, here and now, even though you are so different from Jesus' first hearers or from people elsewhere in the world—people of different cultures, races, classes—who are also hearing the good news right now.

Nowhere is this more important, in our own time, than in the matter of Scripture. For many Christians, the Bible has become a paper tyrant, a rule book written in a strange code, an unalterable and inflexible law. For such people, Christianity has ceased to be good news. Instead, they make it an occasion of cruelty toward themselves and an instrument for controlling or repressing those who are different—less pious, less respectable, than they.

This sort of legalism threatens to bury the good news. But, when freed from its grasp, the scriptures have much to give. Being written documents, they have survived and kept their shape more exactly than the spoken word. They give us a chance to join in conversation with people who lived long before us, including some people who were close in time to Jesus' ministry. They embody the message of the good news in ways that can still surprise and teach and delight us if we let them.

Christians speak of Scripture as "the Word of God," meaning that God has something to tell us through Scripture—the same good news that God tells us through the supreme Word of God, incarnate in Jesus. The Word of God in the Bible ultimately has only one message to tell: the good news of Jesus. We can expect to find this message not only in the gospels, with their account of Jesus' words and actions, but in Scripture as a whole, if we read it with this hope in mind.

Like any written document, though, the Bible can be read with a variety of different expectations. There is nothing in the Bible itself that says it can be read in only one way. You can read it expecting good news—or you can read it expecting a host of other things such as history, story, scientific explanations, geographic knowledge, law, weapons to hurl at your opponents, spiritual advice, prediction of the future. You can even expect to find bad news for yourself or others. If you expect it, you'll find it. Many have.

Some people (often called "fundamentalists," though they go by other names as well) have mined Scripture for rules of belief and behavior, rules by which they seek to bind themselves and others, rules which they can and do use in a hard and narrow fashion. Their way of reading Scripture is easy, but it's wrong—wrong because it severs the Bible from the good news, and therefore from Jesus himself and from the God of Jesus.

Such a reading of Scripture, in fact, makes of it an idol, another of these little godlings that offer their worshipers a chance to feel in control. They think it gives them a system for earning God's love by being extremely good and respectable or, if that fails, by feeling extravagantly sinful and guilty. This "opportunity," as is always true of idolatry, really turns out to be a kind of slavery. Fundamentalism is a religion that demands sacrifice after sacrifice, including the sacrifice of generosity, openness, hope, love, and, finally, of all ordinary human feeling. This cannot be what Jesus aimed at. Nor is it the reason why the church gathered the scriptures together in the first place.

For Christians, only God is supreme—the God who has addressed us with the good news of forgiving love. The Bible has no authority independent of this God. We go to the Bible with God's good news in mind, expecting to meet it there again, to learn more of it, to converse with those who heard it long ago, and to gain new perspective on the good news in our own world.

What is it, then, that we expect to find? We expect to be surprised by what St. Augustine called the "amazing depth" of Scripture: the power of even a familiar text to say the unexpected when we approach it anew. The good news keeps on being *news*. We keep on learning new things about our lives and our world. And we expect to hear, again and again, the assurance of God's improbable forgiving love.

We find these assurances all through the Bible. The story of creation is not a set of eternal rules, prohibiting the wearing of clothes or meat-eating or divorce or homosexuality or whatever you have been told. It is a story of God's generosity—the gift of existence to a whole universe and us in it. The stories of ancient people, of an Abraham or a Rebecca, are not stories about human righteousness or wisdom or vision, but about God's wooing of humanity. The stories of the Exodus from Egypt are not stories about the excellence of Israel, but about God's persistence in love.

The Song of Songs praises erotic love and so celebrates God's creative and enduring love for us. Job and the Psalms give frank pictures of the complexities of our relationship with God, painful times and happy ones alike. The prophetic books tell about the high and low points of God's partnership with Israel in love, their stormy partings of the way, God's enduring faithfulness, and Israel's joyful reunions with its Lover.

The gospels tell about Jesus' ministry, culminating in his death and resurrection. They contain the parables and other astonishing sayings of Jesus. These teachings undercut our certainty about how the world works and how to get on God's good side, and so they open the way for us to hear the good news of God's forgiveness. The gospels tell about Jesus' care for the weak and sick and the pleasure he took in the company of the "wicked"—*our* company. They tell about the integrity and the pain of his death, and about God's unfailing love that raised him from the dead.

Other books in the New Testament tell about the earliest Christians and the struggles they had in trying to understand what the good news meant for them. With great trepidation, Jesus' followers finally decided to admit Gentiles to their number because they felt the good news demanded it. At other times, however, they seem to have compromised with the demands of the world around them, which could not understand or accept the high status that Jesus had given his women disciples. In either case, what we find here is not precise prescriptions for the life of the church in our own age, but insight into the promise and difficulty of living out the good news in changing times.

The value of the Bible, after all, is not that it is perfect. It isn't. Only God is perfect. The value of the Bible is that it's full of good news. It reminds us of God's promises to us. It challenges us to live by faith, hope, and love—in whatever way is uniquely possible and desirable in our own time and place. The Bible is not like a law book to settle all our questions. It is more like a parable to evoke new ones.

Every time our own situation changes, we shall read it with new eyes, in a new way. The earliest Christians had just this experience. They took the scriptures they had (more or less what we now call the Old Testament) and read them in the light of the good news. They were astonished by what they found. The scriptures became new and rich for them. Things they had not understood or even taken seriously before suddenly became significant, while things they had thought primary receded into the background. The whole of the sacred writings turned out to be not so much about law, as they had supposed, but about love.

Not only did the scriptures become new for them; they proved to be life-sustaining as well. They showed that the good news was very old—as old as God's creation of the world or God's calling of Abraham. They showed that the good news was inclusive, extending to Gentiles as well as Jews. They showed that God's way with the creation is constant and coherent—love, first and last.

The scriptures can do equally good things for people today, if we approach them in the Spirit of good news. We are to look not for ways to establish our own superiority, for reasons to condemn others, for rules to serve as stepping stones as we try to climb into God's favor, but rather for reminders of God's goodness, for help in understanding the surprise of God's forgiveness, for encouragement as we learn to live by faith, hope, and love in the new world that the good news of God's love creates in us and around us.

*I*n Matthew's gospel, Jesus cautions people against the religious authorities of his day, who, he says, "bind heavy burdens and set them on people's shoulders and aren't willing to move them, themselves, with one of their fingers" (Matthew 23:4). He says, by contrast, of his own message: "Come to me, all you who are tired out and weighed down, and I'll give you rest. Take my yoke on yourselves and learn from me, because I'm gentle and humble at heart and you'll find rest for your souls. For my yoke is kind and my burden is light" (Matthew 11:28-30).

The Jesus who was about to be crucified cannot have meant this in a merely optimistic way, as if life were always going to be easy for those who respond to the good news. He was talking, rather, about the contrast between the good news and other, tyrannical sorts of religion. Religion that exists only to assure the pious and respectable that they have the inside track with God and to keep the ordinary, impure people out of their way—such religion, whether Christian or other, binds heavy burdens. Even if it claims the authority of the Bible, it is still contrary to what Jesus represents. Jesus' "burden," even if it does not make for a life free from trouble or difficulty or risk, is light. It is nothing more nor less than the unswerving assurance that God loves you and forgives you and is asking for your love in return. This is the message the Bible exists to proclaim.

Good News and the Church

The good news is inherently social. It brings us into a new kind of community with one another. It is not a story of individual souls fleeing to God out of a wicked and transitory world, but a story of individual people discovering that they are loved—and that everyone else is, too. In discovering this, we discover our deep equality and our fundamental relatedness to one another.

Jesus stressed this aspect of the good news in several ways, above all by his own treatment of people. He encouraged women, children, lepers, the sick, ordinary folk—all those who had been overlooked or dismissed by the pious and respectable people of his day. He rejected the pretensions of the self-confident. He taught love: "Love your neighbor as yourself . . . . Love one another." He even arranged for his message to be carried on in a way that required human community.

Jesus could have written books, but he chose not to. He could have had his disciples memorize a fixed message word for word, but we have no convincing evidence that he ever did. Instead, he worked by exposing people to the good news, letting it do its work on them, and then sending them out to expose others.

This may seem to us a careless and sloppy method, but it is the only one that had any real chance of working, of actually preserving and spreading his good news. If we transform good news into a fixed formula or a fixed method or a fixed way of life, it will soon cease to be either good or news.

For one thing, the good news will become a rule. People will compete to see who can keep it most perfectly. The "more successful" (that is, the more pious and respectable) will begin to look down on the "less successful." The "less successful" will turn into a new group of religious and social outcasts just like the ones Jesus came to help in the first place.

For another thing, a fixed message cannot be heard as good news for you, wherever you happen to be—unless you happen, by happy accident, to be in just the same situation as the person to whom it was first addressed. It may *happen* to be phrased in a way that you can easily hear and interpret for yourself, but more likely it won't. Particularly not if it's phrased in language two thousand years old!

From age to age, the good news spreads through living people, who can say, "Here's how it came to me. Perhaps it will find you in a somewhat different way. Let's think it through together. For there is one message of God's forgiving love for everyone, but it becomes as individual as your own life. It is good news for you as well as for me."

The good news is contagious. It is communicated from one person to another by words, by actions, by character, by manner of life. It is communicated when one person catches another's faith and hope and so becomes a new center of the contagion.

So Jesus chose a very human and very social mode of communication. It makes no pretense to some other-than-human kind of absolutism. It doesn't have a crystalline sort of perfection about it—something that can get the message right once and for all and set it in stone. Instead, it points us toward a *human* kind of power and perfection that is to be found in change and growth and maturity, not in static and unchanging simplicity; a power to be discovered in our conversations, our interactions with one another, not in our individual purity and wisdom.

Given all this, it was inevitable that the good news should give rise to a community—one that was made up of people touched by it, responding to it, and learning how to live in the new world that the good news creates. To be faithful, this community also needs to stay open along its borders, to stay in communication with those who do not identify with it, so that the process of "catching" the good news can continue.

*T*he original community of the good news, of course, is the source of the Christian church. And, as most of us already know, the church has had a very mixed history. On the positive side, the church has carried the good news on and kept it available in various ways. It has enshrined its central themes in Scripture, in preaching, in the sacraments of baptism and communion, in creeds. It has lived out the good news in acts of love and service. When it is truly itself, the church is a community of people who are touched deeply by God's generosity and respond with a new and surprising generosity on their own part. The church is people who are sharing the good news they have heard in word and action.

On the negative side, the church sometimes becomes self-absorbed and forgets that it exists only for the sake of the good news and its continued proclamation. Sometimes, the church has even thought that its own existence was the point of Jesus' work. It has thought of itself as the community of the pure and tried to wall itself off from the impure people outside. It has thought of itself as the sole possessor of truth and tried to silence all other voices. It has claimed a monopoly of God's good will and condemned the rest of God's creation to hell. It has used its scriptures and sacraments as clubs to beat other people with. Its behavior has sometimes had more in common with that of the religious authorities Jesus attacked than with that of Jesus himself. At its worst, the church is riddled with hypocrisy and an enemy of the gospel, belonging more to hell than to heaven.

What are we to make of this strange, composite community, with all its good and evil mixed together?

The first thing is to acknowledge the church's humanness. The church, even at its best, is simply the good news as it is experienced and shared by human beings. Even if the good news gives it an element of the divine, it remains fundamentally a human society.

The church's composite nature, mixed of good and evil, belongs not just to the church, but to every human reality in the here and now. Nothing that is human is pure and simple. Every individual is capable of wrongdoing. Every social group is capable of becoming the tool of wrongdoing, even of institutionalized evil.

Whenever the church wants to think of itself as immaculate, infallible, unerringly right or good, completely trustworthy, it falls into a kind of idolatry. When the church tries to be (or worse, merely pretends to be) perfect, it's making an idol of itself. Ironically, one sometimes finds that even the harshest critics of the church are willing to embrace these idolatrous pretensions. If they agree that the church ought to be perfect, they can do a more devastating job of criticizing its very real flaws.

But everything human in this world is mixed, made up of both good and bad. In the case of the church, the good is the good news itself—a supreme good. The bad is pre-eminently hypocrisy (as it was in the devout religious authorities of Jesus' own time). And this hypocrisy is particularly evil because it masquerades as the good news itself.

It will be impossible to produce an absolutely pure church in this world, free from hypocrisy and devoted solely to the good news. Jesus recognized this. In Matthew's gospel, he says that the church is like a wheatfield where some enemy has sown darnel (Matthew 13:24-30). The farmhands want to root up the weeds, but darnel looks very like wheat and the farmer is afraid they will root the wheat up along with the weeds. "Let it be for now," he says, "and we'll separate it all out in the end."

God will be able to separate the good news in the church from the hypocrisy. We have to find ways to live the good news out even in the context of a mixed reality.

To live with and from the good news means living with this mixed reality of the church. We are sustained by the church as a community of faith, hope, and love, while also fighting against its tendency to narrowness and exclusivity, its arrogance and lies, its ability to turn good into a pretext for evil.

There is no formula for living the good news in the church, but here are some guiding principles. Love the church not for itself, however splendid and beautiful its tradition may be, but for the sake of the good news. Receive the church's gifts as gifts from God. Be on the watch for its tendency to absolutize the good news and turn itself into an idol. Expect that there will always be uncertainties in the process of discerning good and bad. Faithful life is possible for the church only insofar as its members hold it to the standard of the good news itself.

*T*he life of the church is best understood as a kind of ongoing conversation between the good news and the realities of human life in a particular time and place. The "conversation" goes something like this: We try to understand what the good news gives us and asks of us in the here and now. We gain, hopefully, some insight into this. We model the life of our church on this insight. Then, because we are human and want solid ground under our feet, we try to make this model of church life permanent and inalterable. In the process, we gradually lose sight of what it originally meant. Then the good news breaks in again from a new angle and we have to rethink it all.

For example, the early Christians created the office of bishop in order to signify the unity of their scattered communities—unity both within the individual congregation and with other congregations across their world, unity that was a gift and expression of the good news. They gave the bishop some authority to embody and protect that unity. A thousand years later, however, Christians found they had bishops with a great deal of authority and no very clear obligation to the good news. What was wrong was not the original institution of bishops, but the detachment of the role of the bishop from its original purpose. Different churches in the West handled the problem in different ways. Some got rid of their bishops. Others reformed the office. Once the problem became apparent, no one was able to leave it untouched.

Eventually, the good news always breaks through anew. It disturbs the comfort of the existing institutions and disrupts the placidity of self-congratulatory Christianity. It tears down some parts of the existing church and rebuilds with a mix of old elements and new. This is not merely a possibility within Christianity; it is both necessary and inevitable. The church is indeed a human community, with all the confusion that implies, and yet it is also the community of the good news—the community that the good news can and does call to account.

*T*he good news is expressed in a variety of ways in the church, above all in word and sacrament and the sharing of gifts. We may hear the good news in the reading of Scripture, in preaching, and in the words of prayer. We receive it sacramentally in the rites of baptism and holy communion. We share it with one another by sharing our gifts in the community.

I've already said something about the nature of the Bible and its relation to the good news. Preaching is the process by which the word of Scripture combines with the word of good news in our own time to become a new proclamation of Jesus' word. The important thing is not so much that it be fine rhetoric, although that doesn't necessarily hurt, but that it speak the good news of God's love in our lives and encourage faith, hope, and love in us.

The great sacramental rites of the Christian religion are also important in sustaining a life of faith, hope, and love. This isn't because they somehow magically transform you. You don't, for example, need baptism to make God love and forgive you. The sacrament of baptism simply takes the good news of God's forgiving love and applies it to each individual person in a very specific way.

Baptism acts physically on the person through the touch of the water, which unmistakably singles out this particular person at this particular moment. It reaches into the soul by evoking the deep-rooted associations of water, signifying death and life, birth and drowning, the old chaos of the sea and the healing orderliness of washing and cleansing. It acts spiritually by its association with the story of Jesus' death and resurrection. In all these ways, it conveys quite graphically the good news of God's love for the specific person being baptized.

Does baptism make a person more pleasing to God? No. Does God love the baptized better than the unbaptized? No. God cannot possibly love anyone better. God has already loved all humanity enough to come wooing us in Jesus. Baptism doesn't make the good news true for us; the good news is already true. Baptism simply embodies the good news for each individual person in a unique, individual, sacramental way.

In the same way, holy communion is God feeding us sacramentally with the very life of Jesus. It isn't a condition of salvation, but reassurance of it. At one point in John's gospel, Jesus says, "Amen, amen, I tell you, unless you eat the flesh of the son of humanity and drink his blood, you don't have life in yourselves" (John 6:53). This may seem to imply that holy communion is a condition of God's love for us. Yet, only a moment later, Jesus says, "The Spirit is what gives life. The flesh does no good at all. The words I've spoken to you are Spirit and are life" (John 6:63). The message of good news is the source of everything else.

It is a life-giving gift to share Jesus' body and blood in the sacrament of communion. Yet it is not the rite by itself that gives this gift. What gives life is the good news embodied in the rite. The Christian community gathers together to celebrate this good news and to be strengthened by it as it is embodied in these tangible, sacramental forms.

Because the gift of baptism mirrors the good news of God's unfailing love, it cannot be repeated because it cannot be lost. It is a vivid sign of the unfailing quality of God's forgiving love, a reassurance that, whatever you may have done, God never turns you away.

Because the gift of communion mirrors the eternal newness of God's unfailing love, it is repeated often. It reassures us vividly that God never ceases nourishing and sustaining us.

The life of the community that celebrates these sacraments is a life of mutual giving and receiving. The early Christians were convinced that the Spirit has a particular care for the church, supplying the community with all it needs. She does so, however, in a peculiar way. The gifts you need she gives to someone else. The gifts you are given are meant for others. The Christian community can live only by the sharing of these gifts (1 Corinthians 12-14).

The church at its best is a community that lives by this kind of sharing, exercising generosity not only within its own circle, but toward outsiders as well. Jesus, after all, came for the outsiders. None of us has any higher claim on God than the claim to God's willing forgiveness. We are all outsiders, miraculously included within the community of the gospel by God's call.

The church at its worst may be arrogant, hypocritical, nar-row, oppressive. The church at its best, however—the church living its true life—is the community of the loved and for-given, created by the message of good news, celebrating that good news in word and sacrament, living by the gifts of the Spirit, shared out generously among all.

Mark, in his way of telling the story of Jesus, has some hum-bling things to tell all subsequent Christians. At one point, early in his ministry, Jesus tells his inner circle of disciples, "You have been given the mystery of God's kingdom; but to those outside everything comes in riddles" (Mark 4:11). And yet, despite this gift, from this moment onward in the Gospel of Mark, the disciples hardly get a single thing right. Peter does identify Jesus correctly as Messiah, but a moment later he completely misunderstands what that means. Jesus even calls him "Satan," at that point, and says that Peter cares about human business, not the business of God (Mark 8:27-38).

By way of contrast, while the disciples are getting every-thing wrong, there are individual outsiders in Mark's gospel who understand quite well! One in particular—a Syrophoeni-cian woman, an unclean Gentile—begs Jesus to cast the de-mon out of her daughter. He refuses. When she continues pleading, he even gets abusive and tells her he has only come for Israelites. He indirectly calls her and other Gentiles "dogs," a very grave insult in that culture. She replies, "Even the dogs get the crumbs from the masters' tables." She tells him that, no matter how he feels about Gentiles, he has no right to exclude them from God's love—and Jesus admits that she's right! "For this speech," he says, "go; the demon has left your daughter" (Mark 7:24-30).

According to Mark, the disciples have everything given to them, but make poor use of it at best. The outsiders are given only riddles, but often succeed in understanding them and hearing the good news in them. Being a Christian doesn't guarantee that you are wise or right or good; *not* being Christian doesn't guarantee that you have it all wrong. The good news is wherever you find it. It visits everyone and offers life to all who hear it. The person you think less favored than you may very well hear it before you do.

The church, then, is not about "getting it right." It is not about the faithful walling themselves off from the rest of the world. Instead, the church is about hearing good news ourselves and sharing it with others. In community with other people who have heard the news, we hope to receive support and encouragement, reminders of the good news we've heard, moments of new insight, the sharing of gifts and the help of friends and counselors as we discern the shape and direction of our lives.

Without these things, isolated in the world, we would find it much harder to live the good news.

In Closing

Hearing the good news is a beginning. The rest of our life forms our response. To trust that God has loved us in this surprising way, to hope that God will go on loving us in this way, to love the One who has sought our love and to love ourselves for our own newly discovered or rediscovered loveliness, to love our world and our neighbor for the same reason—these acts of love form the bones, the skeleton, of life in the good news. We flesh them out in our daily experience of living in faith, hope, and love. As the good news shapes our lives, we and our world will begin to grow rich with the delight that God has intended for us all along.

In this process of living, there is much to be learned and thought through and put into action. Gradually, we begin to get the feel of this new world into which we have entered. Slowly, we begin to discover what it means to be God's beloved. We come to know ourselves as citizens of heaven and begin to risk living that citizenship out, even as resident aliens here and now. Bit by bit, we surrender our idols and learn to tell the truth and rejoice in it. We find out how to live the good news in the context of the church, relying on the encouragement and discernment offered by friends in the faith and calling the church to remember its own commitment to the good news. We learn to stay in conversation with one another and with our forebears in faith. We learn to accept and value the fixed points of sacraments and Scripture as well to prize the surprises of life in the Spirit. We discover with delight that, however old we may be, we go right on growing and changing and maturing by the power of the good news.

This is what the good news makes possible. You don't have to earn your way by being perfect. You don't even have to pretend to be perfect. God has chosen you in love, just as you are. All is forgiven.

A new country lies before you. A new citizenship is yours. The frontier is open. The border guards have been reassigned. No one needs a visa anymore.

Now take risks. Accept your new citizenship. Make a new beginning with God, with yourself, with your world and with your neighbor.

*T*he new life of the good news is like this:

There was a woman who lived in the country in Sonoma County, near Sebastopol. She had no relatives there—not even any close neighbors. The nearest was an elderly man who lived a half-mile away. Behind her house she had a garden, and at the foot of the garden, two apple trees that were her pride and joy.

Once she was called away to care for her only living relative, who was sick and lived very far away. She gave a key
to the elderly man, who promised to look in on her house
every week or so; but he was too infirm to care for her garden. She thought she would be away a few months, but she
was gone for two years. From far away, she heard about
drought and storms.

When at last the woman came home, she found her house
had lost some shingles, and there was a little water damage
inside. Otherwise, things were much as she left them. Then
she went through the house and out into the garden. It was
overgrown with tall grass and nettles. At the foot of the garden were her two apple trees. They were in bloom—at the
height of their bloom, when apple trees look like white
clouds with a touch of pink and the petals are just beginning
to fall and carpet the ground with white as well.

She stood there awhile and drank it all in, and her heart
filled with delight and thanks. Then she unlocked the tool-
shed, took out her pruners and, wading through the weeds,
went down to the apple trees and began cutting out dead-
wood. And she thought of the day when she would have ap-
ples for herself and her neighbor.

Scriptural Index